Cinema Eden

Cinema Eden

Essays from the Muslim Mediterranean

JUAN GOYTISOLO

Translated by Peter Bush

ELAND
London

First published by Sickle Moon, an imprint of Eland,
61 Exmouth Market, London EC1R 4QL in 2003

From *Aproximaciones a Gaudí en Capadocia* © Juan Goytisolo 1990
(Aproximaciones a Gaudí en Capadocia, Los derviches giróvagos,
Fuerte como un turco, La ciudad de los muertos,
La ciudad palimpsesto, El culto popular a los santos)

From *De la ceca a la Meca* © Juan Goytisolo 1997
(Patrimonio oral de la humanidad, El cine Edén, Genet en Larache)

Translation © Peter Bush 2003

ISBN 1 900209 16 0

Cover designed by Robert Dalrymple
Cover Image: Street performer eating
and breathing fire at night, Marrakech
© Steve McCurry / Magnum Photos

Text set in Great Britain by Antony Gray
Printed in Spain by GraphyCems, Navarra

Contents

MOROCCO

The Oral Patrimony of Humanity

A s BAKHTIN SHOWS in his remarkable study of the world and
writing of Rabelais, there was a time when the real and the
imaginary mingled, names supplanted the things they designated and
newly invented words were wholeheartedly put to use: they grew,
broadened out, shacked up, gave birth like creatures of flesh and
blood. Markets, squares, public spaces constituted the ideal place for
their festive germination. Discourses entangled, legends lived, the
sacred was the target of wiseacres but remained sacred, the bitterest
parodies rubbed shoulders with liturgy, a well-knit story kept its
audience in suspense, laughter preceded the prayers to reward the
bard or showman as the plate was handed round.

The universe of cheapjacks and charlatans, beggars and water-
sellers, tinkers and artisans, cutpurses at their nimble-fingered knavery,
street urchins, lunatics, women of scant virtue, rustics as keen as
mustard, striplings not tarrying to prosper, *pícaros*, cartomancers,
quacks, preachers, doctors of homespun science, that entire motley
world of free-and-easy commerce, once the succulent marrow of
Christian and Islamic society – much less differentiated than people
think in the days of the Archpriest of Hita – was swept away gradually or
at one foul swoop by a nascent bourgeoisie whose State gridironed
cities and lives, and lingered on as a hazy memory in their technically
advanced and morally empty nations. The empire of cybernetics
and the audiovisual flattens minds and communities, disneyises
children, atrophies their powers of imagination. Today only one city

upholds the privilege of sheltering the extinct oral patrimony of humanity, labelled contemptuously as 'Third World' by many. I refer to Marrakesh and the square of the Djemaa el Fna, next to which, on and off for some twenty years, I have joyously written, meandered and lived.

Its bards, performers, acrobats, comedians, storytellers are, more or less, equal in number and quality as on the day when I arrived, or at the time of Canetti's fertile visit or as in the Tharaud brothers' travel account written sixty years earlier. If we compare its present appearance with photographs taken at the beginning of the Protectorate, the differences are few: buildings are more solid, still modest; an increase in wheeled transport; a vertiginous proliferation of bicycles; identical workshy horses and traps. The groups around horse-traders still mix with the *halca* framed by the steam wafting hospitality from the cooking-pots. The immutable minaret of the Koutubia surveys the glories of the dead and the helter-skelter of the living.

In the brief lapse of a few decades the wooden huts with bazaars, cold drinks and second-hand book stalls appeared and disappeared: finished off by a fire, they were moved to the burgeoning New Market (only the booksellers suffered cruel exile to Bab Dukala where they withered and died). The coach companies located on the vertex of Riad Zitun – a ceaseless bustle of travellers, traders and hawkers of tickets, cigarettes and sandwiches – also departed elsewhere with their musical incentives: to the orderly, spick and span bus station. In honour of GATT, the Djemaa el Fna was tarmacked, swept, spruced up: the stalls that punctually invaded its space and vanished in a trice after a glimpse of the watch migrated to more favourable climes. The square lost a little of its hassle and hullabaloo, but retained its authenticity.

Death in the meantime brought natural losses to the ranks of its most distinguished offspring. First went Bakshish, the clown with the tasselled bonnet, whose daily performances drew to the insular orb of his *halca* a tightly-packed ring of onlookers, adults and children. Then, Mamadh, the bike artiste, springing from handlebars to seat, spinning swiftly round in his magical balancing-act. Two years ago it knocked on the door of Saruh (the Rocket), majestic seer and wily goliard, reciter of tasty stories of his own creation about the innocent and cunning Xuhá: deployer of a broad, unblushing language, his allusive and elusive tropes quivered like arrows round their unnamable sexual bull's eye. His imposing figure, shaven skull, pontifical paunch, were inscribed in an ancient tradition of that place, incarnated years ago by Berghut (the Flea) and their origins go back to rougher, harsher times, when rebels and betrayers of the sultan's august authority hung exemplarily from bloody hooks or swayed before a silent, cowered people on the sinister 'swing of the brave'.

In a more recent past, I was belatedly informed of the accidental death of Tabib al Hacharat (the Insect Doctor), to whom Mohamed al Yamani devoted the finest of essays in the magazine *Horizons Maghrebins.* We habitués of the Djemaa el Fna were well-acquainted with that little man and his unruly wisps of hair who, in ever rarer public appearances, tottered around the edges of the square snorting like an asthmatic locomotive beneath the arcades with their cheap cafés and friendly aromas. His life-story, a mixture of truth and legend, rivalled Saruh's: he had likewise chosen the way of vagabond poverty, passed nights in cemeteries and police-stations, spent brief periods in prison – which he nicknamed 'Holland' – for being drunk and disorderly and, when he grew tired of Morocco, so he said, he wrapped a scarf round his possessions and left for 'America' – that is, the waste land next to the Holiday Inn. His verbal humour, tales of fantasy, wordplay, palin-dromes, were unconsciously linked to Al Hariri's *Makamat* – lamentably ignored by the ever dozy and dilatory official Hispanic Arabists – and shared a literary territory that, as Shirley Guthrie was quick to see, connects his outlandishness with the 'aesthetic of risk' of Raymond Roussel, the surrealists and OULIPO. His parodies of the television news, his recipe for the biggest hotpot in the world, spiced by ritual questions to his audience, are models of inventive wit.

I can't resist a mention of his lines about the therapeutic qualities of products he recommended to his audience: no 'love juices', no 'carrot cream' like the official healers, but grated glass or amber extract from the devil's backside . . .

'What about coal?'

'Just the job for eyes, for the agate tap in the iris, for the gyrating beam in the ocular lighthouse. Put coal on your ailing eye, let it get to work till it bursts, get a seven inch nail, drive it in the socket and when it's steady in your hand you'll see thirty-seven light years away.

If you've got fleas in your belly, rats in the liver, a turtle in your brain, cockroaches on the knee, a sandal, a piece of zinc, a twist of gunpowder, I found a sock in the house of one of Daudiyat's wives. Guess where I found it!'

'Where?'

'In a teacher's brain!'

(Translation by Mohamed al Yamani)

But the most serious loss, during Ramadan last year, was the surprise closing down of Café Matich: though a lot of water has flowed since – heavy rains, flash floods and real – the Djemaa el Fna has yet to come to terms with the blow. How do you define the undefinable, the protean nature and all-embracing warmth rejecting any reductive label? Its strategic position, on the busiest corner in the square, made it the hub of hubs, its real heart. An eagle eye from there encompassed the whole realm and treasured its secrets: quarrels, encounters, greetings, con-tricks, furtive groping or gleeful poking, tale-telling, insults, itinerant hum of the blind, gestures of charity. Jostling of crowds, immediacy of bodies, space in perpetual movement comprising the boundless plot of a film without end. The seedbed of stories, hive of anecdotes, pageant of morality tales crowned by a clothes-peg were the daily diet of the addicted. Gathered there were *gnaua* musicians, schoolmasters, college teachers, stallholders, raunchy roughs, small traders, big-hearted rogues, sellers of loose cigarettes, journalists, photographers, atypical foreigners, the local down-and-outs. All levelled by the straightforward manners of the place. In Matich everything was talked about and nobody was shocked. The ruler of this roost possessed a weighty literary culture and the intermittent attentions he paid his customers only surprised newcomers, enraptured as he was by an Arabic translation of Rimbaud.

It was where I lived the crystallised tension and devastating bitterness of the Gulf War, a harsh, unforgettable forty days and forty nights. The tourists had disappeared from the horizon and even veteran residents, with the exception of a handful of eccentrics, no longer ventured there. An old *gnaui* master listened to news of the disaster, his ear up against his portable radio. The panoramic terraces of the Glacier and Café de France were desperately deserted. A red sun, heralding the massacre, bled at twilight, prophetically staining the square.

It was also there I spent the most poetic, light-hearted of New Year's Eves. I sat outside the Matich with a group of friends, awaiting, warmly clad, the advent of the new year. Suddenly, as in a dream, an unloaded cart swung round the corner, on its riding seat a young lad hard put to keep himself upright. His glazed eyes dallied on a blonde girl relaxing by one of the tables. Entranced, he slackened his grip on the reins and the cart slowly ground to a standstill. As if in a slow-motion scene from a silent film, our humble charioteer saluted his belle, invited her to climb into his boneshaker. Finally he got off, walked hesitantly over and, with a laboured *madam, madam*, repeated his seigneurial flourish, the majestic invitation to his Rolls or royal carriage, his lordly landau. The solicitous clientèle warmed to his endeavour, his old clothes transmuted to finery, the vehicle bearing his ephemeral glory. But someone intervened to end the idyll and escorted him to his place. The youth couldn't break the spell, looked over his shoulder, threw kisses and, seeking consolation from this fiasco, patted the thighs of his mare with a touching tenderness (to a chorus of laughter and encores). Then he tried to clamber onto the driver's seat, managed it with some effort and immediately fell backwards on the empty boards, curled up in a ball (to a fresh round of applause). Various volunteers hoisted him up and holding the reins, he blew a goodbye kiss to the Scandinavian deity before disappearing at a brisk trot over the dirty, oblivious tarmac, in a melancholy mood of paradise denied. I had not enjoyed such a scene since the happy days of Chaplin's films: such delicacy, oneiric, alive with humour, deliciously romantic.

Once the café closed down, we habitués scattered like a diaspora of insects deprived of their nest. The *gnaua* gather at night on the inhospitable asphalt or meet up in the backroom of an old *fonduk* on Derb Dabachi. The rest of us come to terms as best we can with the demise of that international centre of cultures, reliving episodes and moments from its mythical past splendours, like nostalgic emigrés in the makeshift shelters of exile. But the Djemaa el Fna resists the combined onslaught of time and an obtuse, grubby modernity. The *halcas* don't fade, new talents emerge and an audience hungry for stories crowds gleefully round its bards and performers. The space's incredible vitality and digestive capacity glues together what is scattered, temporarily suspends differences of class and hierarchy. The tourist-laden coaches which, like whales, flounder there are immediately wrapped in its fine web, neutralized by its gastric juices. This year the nights of Ramadan assembled tens of thousands in its centre and roadways, around the portable cookers, and raucous bargaining over shoes, clothes, toys and bric-a-brac. In the glow from the oil lamps, I thought I noticed the presence of the author of Gargantua, of Juan Ruiz, Chaucer, Ibn Zayid, Al Hariri, as well as countless goliards and dervishes. The tawdry image of the fool slavering over his mobile phone neither tarnishes nor cheapens the exemplary brilliance of the domain. The dazzling incandescence of the word prolongs its miraculous reign. But sometimes I am worried by the vulnerability of it all and my lips tremble fearfully with a single question: 'For how long?'

Cinema Eden

THERE EXISTS AN ALMOST EXTINCT SPECIES of cinema whose auditorium, dense atmosphere and original setting stand out more strongly, more glowingly in the memory than the meandering plot of their films. My childhood experience was decisive in this respect and casts light on my future fondness for the flea-pits that recall those first cinemas I patronised in the neighbourhood of the district of Barcelona where I was born and to which I returned with my stricken family a few months after Franco's victory. These were the *Murillo* – the *Primavera* from the prewar years – a name it reclaimed in the fifties before being closed down for good and re-placed by an apartment block at the point where paseo Bonanova crosses calle Anglí– and the smaller, humbler *Breton*, right in the heart of the still rather prim and provincial suburb of Sarrià. Their audi-ences were mainly young and enthusiastic: they gathered or queued up in front of the box-office ages before the programme started and whetted their appetite by gazing at the posters and photos advertising the films for that day and the weeks to come, rapturously consuming lupin seeds and garishly coloured sweets through lips coated black by prolonged sucking of gluey sticks of liquorice. On the inside, the stalls and tatty upstairs had more the look of a shed or barn than a real cinema. The noisy, unruly film-goers watched the compulsory round of newsreels, first the *UFA*, translated from German, and then the *Nodo*, in which the Wermacht's unstoppable advances and the Caudillo's appearances were greeted by the adults, up on their feet, arms raised in salute. And finally, the horror, adventure or cowboy films that were to carry on throughout the school year with little variation: the spectators were not after novelties; on the contrary, they came to be excited by situations and subjects that were familiar. We were bored by sentimental films aimed at a female audience and avoided them: we migrated from the *Murillo* and its mixed clientèle to take refuge in the *Breton*. I remember how we came out of the place in a daze, still entranced by the magic emanating from the screen, arguing with some friend over the hero of the film's feats of daring and the moments of greatest danger or tension. In that period, alone or with my brothers, I would walk to the cinema and only very occasionally took the Sarrià metro, in order to alight at the Gracia and Catalonia stations, on my way to the *Roxy*, *Vergara* or *Capitol*. The elegant *Montecarlo* had yet to be inaugurated, and the luxurious *Windsor*, whose sanctuary I would set foot in much later, in the pretentious guise of a gilded youth, did not yet exist.

*   *   *

Over the last thirty years, in cities throughout the world, I have come across cinemas, like those I knew as a child, where the atmosphere inside is equally if not more inviting than the programme of films: the *Luxor* and *Palais Rochechouart* in Paris, the *Vox* in Tangier, the *Caruso* in Essaouira, the *Belkis* in Aden and, above all, in Marrakesh: the *Rif*, the *Mabruka*, the *Mauritania*, the *Eden*.

The *Luxor* – to which I devoted a few pages of my novel *Makbara* – was a real cinema-palace, with one-price seats in the stalls, circle and gods, where the motley audience displayed only a passing interest in what was happening on the screen: for many, the real action was to be found in the basement and circle toilets, the back rows of the *mezzanine* and the whole of the gods. The regulars were largely North Africans with a faithful minority of heterogeneous gays, from a painted lady from Cadiz complete with fan and mantilla to the semiologist Roland Barthes. Some of those customers hadn't a clue about the story-line of the occasionally fascinating films that were shown in the cinema: their minds lay elsewhere. When an intrepid compatriot extended her manual activities into the centre of the stalls and was caught in the act by the usherette's torch, she responded in queenly style to the man marching her out: 'But *that's* what I come for. You don't think I buy a ticket because of the divine quality of your films!'

Numerous legends are in circulation about the *Mabruka* cinema in Marrakesh, situated close to the main square of the Djemaa el Fna. The mass of youths jostling outside to get into the double bill of Wild West and Kung-Fu films enables the nimblest and sharpest wits to 'swim' the crawl over the heads of their companions en route to the box-office and horizontal purchase of their ticket! According to eye-witness reports, the day a deluge fell on the city and a torrent of water from the square flooded the cinema, the audience didn't budge: they removed their shoes and crouched on the seats till the flood-level reached twenty centimetres when it was necessary, to a hale of insults and protests, to evacuate the place. The most exaggerated accounts maintain some people stayed on impassively watching the film, with water up to their necks!

*   *   *

The *Eden* cinema concentrates within its walls all the virtues and attractions of the flea-pits I have mentioned. Its privileged location by the arch or funnel of the bustling thoroughfare of Riad-Zitun al Yedid and its large yard overlooking games rooms with table football and one-armed bandits, cold-drink shops and parking space for mopeds and bicycles, create a huge, variegated territory, of which the flea-pit as such is but the key feature, the *holy of holies*. While the crowd proceeds through the entrance, window-gazers, hypnotised by the posters, obstruct the traffic and provoke snarl-ups in which the drivers' angry tooting merges with motorcyclists' insults, pedestrians' shouts and the resigned or humorous comments of people living in the neigh-bourhood. The whirlwind appearance of street-hawkers with huge plastic sacks containing their merchandise, fleeing from a posse of municipal police, adds to the cheerful, ferocious chaos, the daily apotheosis of confusion. Usually, it flows smoothly: the hired carriages move forward impetuously to the shout of *balek, balek,* alerting the unwary cyclists who ziz-zag their way boldly and swiftly through the mass. Heavily laden donkeys stoically tolerate the points of their masters' goads but, in the midst of the tumult, the inquisitive, dreamy-eyed passers-by, cyclists, car-drivers and coachmen linger a few moments on the *Eden* cinema posters, drawn by the magnetic scenes of love and violence, at the risk of causing serious accident. But God throws his mantle of mercy over the city and cases of injury or bruising are miraculously rare.

Sellers of almonds and peanuts, hard-boiled eggs, violently coloured sweets and nougat or loose cigarettes line up against the wall by the entrance to the yard. In the interval, the doors stays closed and the spectators are jammed against the wrought-iron gate, poking their arms between the bars, to purchase, after scraping the bottoms of their pockets, savoury cornets, rolls, a humble *Marquise* or a lordly, much coveted, *Marlboro.* From the outside, the scene of jostling and begging hands inevitably reminds one of prisons. But the cinema management has no truck with smart-arses or -alecs and the incarcerated audience benefits from the break to quench their thirst or appease their hunger, play a game of table football, relieve themselves. The men go indis-criminately into the gents or ladies: there is a conspicuous absence of female cinema-goers. No woman, whether alone or accompanied, would ever think of entering the rough, tightly-packed space of the *Eden* cinema. Only two or three girls from the square, sporting shirts, jeans and male hair-styles – who have abandoned their previous restricted status for the freedom enjoyed by the other sex – go to the flea-pit where they are never molested. Their new colleagues show unanimous respect for such a bold, unusual decision.

When the show is over and the movie-goers rush into the street, numerous spectators, still mesmerised, take a last look at the posters for the films they have just seen, as if to confirm the reality of the fleeting world to which they have been transported and where suddenly they no longer belong.

*   *   *

The programmes in the cinema usually include two films: a Hindu melodrama and a Karate film. Sometimes the latter is replaced by a Western and the former by a bland item of soft porn. The nature of what is being projected can be easily guessed from the street: the ratatatat of machine-gun fire and thud of bullets would be enough to raise the dead; the moans of pleasure of the artist in her underwear, up on the screen for public consumption, mingle with the roars of a randy audience; a mellifluous melody, reinforced by a piping voice, reveals the lonely melancholy of the protagonist of the Hindu film.

The *Eden* cinema regulars enjoy flitting from American or Taiwanese violence to the magic and mystery of Indian productions. As inhabitants of the city are aware, the cinema shares the same owner as the *Regent* in the Europeanised district of Gueliz. A skinny little fellow, of undefinable age, bikes the reels over daily from one place to the other. His punctuality is proverbial and the films transported from the *Regent* are shown at the *Eden* right on schedule.

One day, however, the errand boy didn't arrive: it was later discovered he had been involved in a traffic accident. But the Hindu film was nowhere to be seen and gradually impatience led the frustrated spectators into choppier waters: shouts, whistles, howls of

anger raised the tempo and some youths were already threatening to
pull the place apart. Faced by the dilemma of dealing with a riot or
warning the police, the cinema manager climbed on to the stage and
confronted the audience: the Hindu film had been delayed but he
could offer another in exchange that would be to their liking. An all-
action Western. Unmoved by the offer, the aroused gathering
drummed on the wooden backs of their seats to the tune of: *Hindi!*
Hindi! Neither promises nor bravado could sooth the serried ranks
deprived of their favourite film. After consultations and referenda
more intricate than any Geneva peace negotiations, the parties
involved reached an agreement: everybody present would get a free
pass to a showing of the film the day after. Though more efficient
than the general secretary of the UN and the highly respected
Community representative in the present conflict in the Balkans, the
names of the architects of that historic truce are not recorded in the
neighbourhood annals!

*   *   *

In the early sixties I regularly attended the first releases of karate films.
In those years I was giving my courses on literary theory at New York
University and the birth of the genre allowed me to analyse its various
structures following Propp's classic study of the morphology of the
Russian folk-tale.* The subject had yet to be cast into an unchangeable
code and, like the first Westerns in which protagonists were identified
by possession or lack of a moustache or the colour of their shirt –
white for the clean-shaven hero and black for the hairy outlaw – it
hovered between several options, moving tentatively forward till it was
locked into ritual by the starry brilliance of Bruce Lee: synchronised

---

* *Morphology of the Folk Tale* by Vladimir Propp (University of Texas Press,
   Austin; 1968)

confrontations between rival gangs, the prodigious leaping and vaulting of the karatekas, the elimination one after another of the enemy from bottom to top of their hierarchical pyramid. At the packed Sunday matinée performances on Barbès and Pigalle, I confirmed on my return to Europe the reduction of the *ars combinatoria* of elements to a minimum of possibilities and the choreographed patterning of the fights conceived and executed with all the ceremonial formality of ballet.

My North African friends enjoyed this as much as I did. The Manichaeism of the films with their clear distinction between good and bad helped them escape briefly from a world in which the blurred frontiers between exploiters and exploited hid the real reasons for their exile and alienation. As I checked out the genre's rules of the game, they celebrated and applauded the predictable feats of the winner. But, although of a different nature, my interest was real and harmonised with that of the immigrants in a warm and binding communion. Every artistic genre engenders its own parody and the parody of karate soon showed its face. Some anarchists imbued with the festive spirit of May '68 acquired the rights to a Taiwanese film, adapted the sound-track to their own taste and managed to infiltrate the network of local cinemas mainly visited by immigrant workers. Its title, *The Dialectic Can Break Stones*, was, it seems, an imitation of one of Mao's famous dictums. The pirated plot went something like this: out-and-out war pits two gangs of youths against each other, the *bureaucrats* against the *libertarians*. The leader of the latter – we'll call him Ling Pi – goes out alone to fight off twenty of the enemy armed to the teeth. His little sister Miu wants to fight alongside him, but our hero puts a stop to that: 'Your mistaken political line won't let you come with me. Stop reading the mind-numbing pair Marx and Lenin and get into the complete works of de Sade!' The girl departs sobbing her heart out to take refuge in the family home. 'Why are you crying, Miu?' her father asks anxiously. 'Ling Pi wouldn't let me go with him to liquidate the bureaucrats. He says I lack political maturity, and shouldn't waste my time on the Communist classics, I would do better to study de Sade.' 'Quite right too, my dear Miu. A girl would get much more from reading *The Last Hundred Days of Sodom* than anything written by that turn-off Marx.' The following sequence shows Ling Pi, in full possession of his martial arts, as his forearm chops its way through the ranks of bureaucrats: 'You idiots, stop parroting Marchais's editorials from *L'Humanité!*' The leader of the enemy: 'Revisionist, traitor!' Ling Pi: 'Now you'll find out about the muscle-power of a pupil of Nietzsche and Lou Andrea Salomé!' etc. Needless to say, I was delighted by the film. But it also delighted the rest of the spectators who, absorbed in the wondrous action, didn't pay much attention to the sparkling wit of the dialogue. If I'm not mistaken, Tono and Miura carried out a similar kind of plot-switch with an old Viennese film that they called *A Moustache for Two*. In both cases, the humour hit home and refuelled the theories for my courses on narrative structure, which had hitherto centred on the romances of cloying Barbara Cartland and the epic tale of the unvanquished James Bond.

*   *   *

My fondness for Hindu films came later. On my first stays in Marrakesh, before I settled down in the neighbourhood around the Djemaa el Fna, I rented a small house in the Kasbah district, whose only cinema still survives and retains the name of *Mauritania*. It was the enchanted world of films produced in the studios of New Delhi and Bombay, the factory of dreams aimed at an impoverished, semi-illiterate public. The twists in the plot transported us to the universe of the so-called Byzantine novel, with its kidnappings, disappearances, anagnorisis, lonely lovers' ballads, miraculous encounters of characters in the most unlikely places. The songs of the hero or heroine separated by adversity played a decisive role in the sound-track, and moved the audience, which didn't understand a word. The anodyne Arabic and French subtitles took up half the screen but few spectators bothered to follow them. What happens in these films really doesn't require erudite commentaries and exegesis.

The scene in which the imprisoned bride sings of her anguish in the depths of the wilderness, her heart-breaking lament spanning thousands of kilometres to reach the ears of her lover and bring floods of tears to his eyes, was particularly appreciated. The script-writers add to the panoply of fictional devices employed by Lope de Vega and Cervantes a range of supernatural ingredients: spells, potions, portents, levitations, celestial punishment in the form of devastating lightening. Two children lost in the middle of the jungle are pointed homewards thanks to opportune advice – in bilingual translation – from a humble cow! An orphan-laden elephant stops to consult the signposts at the crossroads and finally chooses the right one while enormous tears sparkling with happiness stream down its wrinkly skin!

I have to confess that these films interested me and still interest me much more than the usual realistic/psychological productions from Europe and America. Their narrative codes, open to all manner of coincidence and surprise, are quite refreshing after the insipid diet of consumer pap colonising our screens and televisions. The *Eden* cinema regulars prefer to revel in the wonders and prodigies tradition-ally attributed to the saints as if compensating for their cruel loss and consequent deprivation. I remember the plot but not the title of the best Hindu film shown there. A rich parvenu is having a palace-warming with much pomp and ceremony. 'My lucky star protects me from any kind of danger', he exclaims. Destiny belies his predictions, seconds later: an earthquake! The house collapses around him apparently burying his family and guests in the ruins. The sole survivors are his wife and one of his children who, years later as an adult, joins the police force in order to try to support his mother. The young policeman succeeds in arresting a famous bandit and taking him to court. The criminal is defended before the judge by a lawyer to whom he recounts his life story. The lawyer and policeman are moved by his tale and their emotion infects the prosecuting magistrate: the accused is his brother and the four of them are linked unknowingly by blood-ties! Moles, scars and other bodily signs corroborate the truth of their discovery: sobs, embraces, tears all round! The trial is suspended and the reunited family goes out into the street. 'How happy our father would be if he could see us now!' the widow sighs. No sooner said than done: a close-up of a blind beggar walking towards the courtroom with his stick and begging bowl. The deceased! Mother, policeman, outlaw, lawyer, magistrate and beggar weep and embrace. End of film. That day I was the only one to rise to my feet and applaud, but I did so with such vigour that I soon carried most of the audience with me.

*   *   *

The *Eden* cinema is an old, down-at-heel flea-pit. The columns supporting the gods – it would be incongruous to call it the circle – are in the middle of the auditorium and obstruct the view of those unlucky enough to be seated behind them, forcing them to lean left- or rightwards much to the annoyance of their neighbours. Peanut husks, though swept up at the end of each show, very soon cover the cement floor and crack when trodden on by people changing seat, coming in, or going out on their way to the games and toilets. The heavy atmosphere, saturated with tobacco smoke and kef, seems both to glue the audience together and stick to it. The spectators upstairs throw their empty boxes and cones into the stalls and ignore the insults that drift upwards. One afternoon, a drunk urinated on the front stalls and a punishment detail expelled him militarily into the street. In the karate and action films, the violence spreads to the public and the bigger, stronger youths unceremoniously evict others from their favourite seats. In an atmosphere like a wild animals' den – acrid smells, sweat, jostling – the gun shots and bellowing of the karatekas trigger off howls of delight or angry whistles verging on insurrection. But the overflowing waters return to their rightful channel. During the showing of films made in India, the audience remains silent and witnesses in fascination the lament of the heroine kidnapped by pirates or the over-layering on the screen of the lovers' levitating dance, united though their love is so long-distance. The poisoning of a newly-born child by a witch, its miraculous resurrection and the implacable punishment meted out are welcomed with curses and cheers. The public will not tolerate sad endings or the victory of evil. The cinema's battered fire-fighting equipment couldn't prevent the place being burnt down. Aware of the dangers, and to stave off possible rioting, the management only selects films which end happily.

*   *   *

At eleven o'clock at night, the half-empty streets suddenly become animated. The youngsters leave the cinema *en masse,* as if on an unruly, warlike demonstration. The seller of hard-boiled eggs, the stall selling sweets and cakes, the cigarette retailer hurriedly dispatch their merchandise. A mobile kebab vendor sends up smoke signals a few metres from the cinema and is besieged by ravenous filmgoers. The noisy cassette shops have shut and the clientèle of the *Eden* scatter in silence to face the harsh realities of their lives, rubbing their eyes as if they have just woken up.

The Poet Buried at Larache

> Every man seeks more or less consciously to put forward an image of
> himself which will spread far and wide and after death in order to
> wield power or else irradiate a strength that is at once gentle,
> powerful and giving : this image once detached from man
> or group or act makes people say that they are exemplary.
>
> JEAN GENET, *A Prisoner of Love*

SIX YEARS AFTER HIS DEATH and the posthumous publication
of his most beautiful and boldest work, the figure and literary
enterprise of Genet still arouse bitter polemic: they are alive. The
virulence of some attacks shows how his provocative personality
and the moral and aesthetic radicalism shaping his work struck bull's
eye. Those who are scandalised by them, swathed in the virtuous
cloak of Polite Society and Correct Thinking, are precisely the ones
he was aiming at: his declared enemies. That's why the hypocrisy,
conventionality and narrow-mindedness displayed by some critics fit
perfectly in his writing as the voices of the officers, judges, ladies and
clerics who speak out in *The Maids*, *The Balcony* or *The Blacks*. If some
malevolent genie replaced their assertions or ripostes with paragraphs
from the press cuttings of *A Prisoner of Love* or *L'ennemi déclare*, it's
unlikely anyone would notice. Genet gallantly allows his adversaries
to chit-chat within his own inner space: he invites them to get up on
stage.

But beyond the inane verbiage destined to become fodder for

erudite investigation, an image different to the one desired or unconsciously sought after by the poet in the various phases of his life is
perhaps beginning to take shape, is gradually becoming clearer as if on
a photographic negative or plate. This fixed, definitive image of man
and artist, inaccessible unless we depart crass reality and enter the
universe of absence, becomes visible out of nothingness, from the
shadowy realm of subtlety.

At the colloquium devoted to Genet on the occasion of the revival
of *The Balcony* at the *Grand Théâtre de L'Odéon* in Paris, I referred to
the suggestive paradox he had created when he disappeared from the
world and entered history: that is, how to talk of the grace and
damnation he conferred on those who knew him, which leads us to
use a religious language at odds with his atheism. How can one
reconcile the grace and sanctity I shall later refer to with the Cartesian
rationalism that structures the rigorously egalitarian conception of
humanity which underlies the illusions and deceits of his theatre and
poetic writing? The philosopher's decision to separate the knowable
sciences from those encompassing other areas of man's being (ethics,
society, metaphysical vision etc.), led him to reject differences based
on skin-colour, sex, cultural and religious traditions as incongruous
in the area of natural human reason: in truth black minds and
Catholic mathematics don't exist. This conception, which underpins
Genet's games with mirrors and staging of the great theatre of the
world, eliminated the idea of transcendence and put all religions in
the same bag. Nevertheless, a reading of his works spotlights the
search for an 'immoral' exemplariness forged from a defence of values
and actions universally the object of reproach and censure. To the
rationalist Genet, the implacable destroyer of the principles and
taboos which guide bourgeois society, one must then add another
Genet, whose life and work can be interpreted as a twisting, turning,
sinuous conquest of a subtle form of exemplariness: at first sight a
negative model, but which perhaps attains its real stature once

examined in the light of other paths to secret perfection that flourished more than ten centuries ago in the cultural space of Islam.

When I described in my novel *Landscapes after the Battle* the literary and humane ideal of the eccentric scribe in the Parisian district of Le Sentier, it was quite clear to any reader familiar with my work that I was referring to Genet:

> A man who shuns vanity, scorns the rules of decorum and social convention, seeks no disciples, tolerates no praise. His virtues are kept modestly hidden, and to further conceal them he delights in practices that are contemptuous and base: he therefore not only brings upon himself the reprobation of his fellows but provokes them into ostracising and condemning him.
>
> (translated by Helen Lane)

Scornful rejection of the sympathy or admiration of others, the indifference to reputation of the 'lone man in the crowd', as Ibn Arabi defined the *malamati* gives us one of the essential keys to the last decades of Genet's life. The adepts of *malamiya* – a term derived from *malama* or censure – avoided any expression of piety and on the contrary displayed behaviour that was reprehensible in their neighbour's eyes, in order to hide from the world their mystic state and inner piety. For the same reasons, they refused to be set apart by virtuous acts and preferred to get only backward glances or be treated condescendingly. Jalal al-din Rumi, the sage, poet and founder of the order of the whirling dervishes, submitted meekly to the test set by his friend and mentor, Shams Tabrizi, namely to buy a flask of wine in the busiest market in the locality in order to tame his pride and deliberately cause a scandal. Before him, a *malamati* from among the admirable Persian Sufis advised one of his followers: 'hide your good works as others hide their evil deeds'. The extravagant behaviour of some 'popular saints' in North Africa – their lack of concern for prescribed rituals, public drunkenness, sodomy etc. –

makes up part of the provocation of the self-righteous Pharisees through which they burnished their own hidden virtue. 'If you are able to place yourself in a situation where you are suspected of robbery,' Bishr Ben Al Mariz Al Hafi would say, 'do everything possible to do so.' In spite of their strange excesses Ibn Arabi placed the *malamati* in the highest sphere of sanctity.

The convergences of the bard of theft, betrayal and homosexuality with the Sufi addicts of *malama* are mysterious but undeniable. Although it would be anachronistic and wrong to attribute to a writer of Genet's standing the faith and mysticism of the *malamatis*, we find too many points of contact between him and them to be able to ignore them. Those of us who lived near him for a time and were privileged to observe him could write a whole book about his acts of disloyalty, sudden rages, irrational fits of pique, his broken promises: that provocative violence against all oppressive powers and symbols which naturally turned him into the ideal foil of the society in which he lived. But as well as the details and anecdotes that already make up his legend, we glimpsed some delightful moments of saintliness when unthinkingly he lowered his guard: a saint by distraction, like various *malamatis* he heroically suffered exhaustion and physical pain in order to serve the weak and persecuted, and forgetting his praise of betrayal revealed an unexpected and moving fidelity in moments of painful ordeal. No need to add that such moments, carefully hidden from public view as we hide our cowardice and shameful acts, later aroused in him an often angry reaction to eyewitnesses, as if surprised *in flagrante* committing some unworthy act, he wanted to take revenge on his carelessness and those who might relate it.

Was he striving to compose the image he wanted to spread and even substitute for himself? As he says in one of the most beautiful pages of his posthumous work, was he seeking out, distorting, sketching in unwieldy monsters and aberrations he would have had to destroy if they hadn't fallen apart of their own accord? Did his desire to challenge the hypocrisy of the self-righteous to the bitter end by proudly championing the loathsome and the vile force him to erase from the picture anything that contradicted his infamous reputation? Was he the 'actor and martyr' of Sartre's stodgy book, on the look out for the definitive act that would send him headlong into nothingness, yet would at the same time spur on the collective imagination, if not like a hero, prophet and saint, at least like the great murderers or de Sade's perverse characters? We shall never know.

What we can attest to from the other side of the sea, from North Africa where I write these lines, is the fact that the image forged from his vault into notoriety – still present in the way conformist intellectuals, cultural pundits and the great national flock of his fellow countrymen reject him – is tending to fade and be supplanted by one that is suggestive and poetic. The *nesrani* or European buried in the old Spanish cemetery of Larache, defender of the oppressed and friend of the Palestinian cause, repatriated almost furtively to Morocco as just another migrant worker who died in Europe, has now little in common with the man Cocteau and Sartre knew and who scandalised Parisian literary circles. The image he perhaps wanted to create for himself has faded to the point of extinction and the one emerging from the photographic plate or negative would no doubt surprise any onlooker.

The poet's simple grave, a few metres from a cliff endlessly pounded by waves swept in by the currents in the sea, contrasts in its beauty and the careful attention it receives with its older and more undesirable neighbours, generally members of the Hispanic military caste in Africa, like the one he parodied in some of the unforgettable scenes in *The Screens*, that he would curse night and day – I can imagine his bouts of anger – if he were alive. Anonymous hands deposit posies of flowers, water the surrounding grass, even claim the epitaph as a relic or pious souvenir. Moroccans and Europeans linger there and surround it with a halo of almost saintly respect.

Cinema Eden

Although *ualaya* or saintliness in Islam goes back, as we know, to the first centuries of the Hegira, it does not obey the strict rules and investigation – even in its aberrations – that are imposed by the Church of Rome. The 'friends of God' are freely chosen by the people, and their saintliness, earned in life or after death, is often fortuitous and fragile. Characters who for a time enjoyed the devotion of the faithful later fall into oblivion, and their abandoned, ruined hermitages are pathetic testimony to an irrevocable loss of grace. Others, on the other hand, draw hundreds or thousands to the shrines they or their heirs founded, on the occasion of a pilgrimage or on a particular festival day in the Islamic calendar. In Morocco, some are Hebrew and receive the *ziara* or visit from both Jews and Muslims. Although official Sunnis condemn these hybrid expressions of religiosity, they are forced to accept them after the historic failure of the reformist movement of the *salafia*.

In time, will Genet become one of those 'popular saints' whom pilgrims ply with humble presents and ask for favours after they have attached their offerings to the trees near his grave? It wouldn't be at all out of the ordinary if the magnetism of the final image created by his death were to take on a lasting shape. If one of the 'saints' in the region of Marrakesh was a French soldier in Lyautey's army who fell in love with a village charcoal-burner, embraced Islam and stayed with him until his death, and now grants fertility to some women who visit his grave, doesn't the figure of the ex-*poète maudit* have merits and virtues that aren't any less attractive and conclusive for being modestly hidden? The fascination exercised by this 'lone man in the crowd' has escaped his grasp and may take on unforeseen forms in the realm of legend. Who knows whether his desire to attain control of the 'fabulous, on a small or grand scale' is not now fulfilled: 'To become an eponymous hero, projected in the world as exemplary and, consequently, unique, because he emerges from the evidence and not from status'?

The Popular Worship of Saints in North Africa

THE JOURNEY FROM MARRAKESH TO SI FATMA, in the heart of the Ourika valley, condenses into one hour a whole illustrated course in geography. As the road leaves the walled city and the Agdal Gardens and heads for the fastnesses of the Atlas mountains – now gleaming, whitened by winter snow, now bare and swathed in mist – the flat, half-desert landscape, occasionally adorned with elm trees and lines of cypresses indicating watering-holes and irrigated areas, is enhanced by a subtle range of cleverly combining tones as if painted by an artist: at the entrance to the valley, the sea of olive trees and reddish hue of the earth and villages clustered on the hills evoke the Mediterranean land-scapes of Greece or Sicily; then, as the valley winds and narrows, boxed between mountains, the colour of the soil and beech and fir trees unexpectedly confront us with an almost oneiric vision of Switzerland. In winter, the contrast is abrupt, beautiful; in August, after a flash-flood that swept away several orchards, fields under cultivation and a grotesque chalet with swimming-pool which the Ministry of Culture should have demolished years ago out of a respect for the area and norms of good taste, sadness at the devastation permeates enjoyment in selfish contemplation. Nevertheless, life resurges with panache, small cafés and shops attend to a clientèle of summer visitors and to lorries packed with peasants off to Si Fatma where the annual pilgrimage or *moussem* is to be celebrated over three days.

Cinema Eden

The valley adjacent to the peak where the remains of Lella Fatma are at rest has been transformed into a market-cum-fairground. Despite the difficult location – the fork in the river, the boulders and water-logged fields – the people gathered there wander along paths improvised between kebab stalls, clothes and shoes salesmen, butchers and awnings over candle and spice sellers; yellow and orange bottles, put to cool in the riverbed, glint in the water like shoals of small exotic fish; countrymen in a variety of headdresses and *burnous* strike deals in the patch designated for animals and horses; various *halcas* or rings of bystanders absorb the usual patter of hawkers of talismans or recipes; others, as in the Djemaa el Fna, invite customers to 'fish' from bottles of Coke or Fanta; a boxing-match promoter, after invoking God's generosity in order to extract a few coins from the crowd, threatens the reluctant and the miserly with attacks of madness that can only be cured by the Buya Omar brotherhood: the challenge bears fruit and two mountain lads next to me anxiously start scratching around in the bottoms of their pockets.

Happily, a wood of magnificent walnut trees shades the slope to the hermitage: as the path climbs steeply I watch barbers shaving their customers' skulls as if they were shearing sheep, a band of ageing musicians with rustic instruments, and families and groups of women cooking or camping down in the sweet lethargy of summer. The track zigzags and the line of those walking up crosses those returning from their visit to the saint. Some beggars seek alms at strategic points. When I reach the top and survey the colourful panorama of the pilgrimage on the banks of the river, I spot the hermitage camouflaged behind the foliage of fir trees: a *kubba* of pink-ochre walls topped not by the usual dome, but by the roof and green tiles of so many mosques and saints' holy places in Morocco. The building comprises a porch, where there is a heaped offering of blessed bread, and the tomb itself: the latter, draped with a *kesua* (a covering) of green silk, is surrounded by a bronze or gilt-metal grille.

The faithful reverently touch the bars, walk slowly round the catafalque of Lella Fatma and her two daughters buried there, brush their hands against the stela that act as 'witnesses' and immediately rub their cheeks to receive grace. Some women stay crouching there and one, face up, moans gently, quietly invoking the favour of the saint.

Two days later, on the road from Agadir to Tiznit, the mass of crowds and traffic informs travellers they have arrived at Sidi Bibi. The esplanade surrounding the marabout's *zawiya* and sanctuary offers a spectacle similar to Si Fatma: pilgrims, traders, worshippers have more space here and a group of riders is trying out its gun-skills, firing as they gallop by the platform and tents of local dignitaries and guests of honour. Frail eucalyptus branches offer scant protection against the rigours of the sun. Stalls and bamboo shelters where customers drink tea and recover alternate with the furious roar of fairground stands: dances, theatrical spectacles, the feats of a motorcyclist hanging from the so-called Wall of Death. A transvestite in a red caftan sways his hips and bounces his breasts as a stall-owner touts the merits of his cooking-range.

In the space reserved for the *halca*, a bearded, one-armed member of the brotherhood of the Aisauas, wearing simple knee-length breeches yet clad in a halo of rugged beauty prods at a box full of snakes, wrapping them round his bare shoulders as if they were garlands from Hawaii, sticks out his tongue, runs its tip along the most elastic, agitated, slenderest part of what is apparently a viper, blessed with the powers of the founder, Sidi Hadi Benaisa, who, it is said, possessed the gift of taming wild animals and subduing malign serpents.

The tomb of Sidi Bibi is in the precinct of a *zawiya* with a court-yard, a well from which holy water is drawn and a mosque of modest proportions. Overall it is in keeping with the rural model of a holy place with its whitewashed walls, *kubba* and white domes, crenellations and towers painted a naïve pink and green. The faithful make their way through the poor gathered round the generous saint and queue at the door to the hermitage which shelters his remains. The offerings of the devout – hundreds of candles of every shape and size that will burn throughout the year in honour of Sidi Bibi – are heaped on a salver. A young man, naked from the waist up, carries a prickly pear over his shoulder, his chest and arms bristling with prickles. Men and women kiss the *kesua* over the catafalque, murmur prayers and promises, give alms to the old and infirm. The people working in the *zawiya* swing censors and the smell of benzoin or another aromatic balsam mysteriously seems to calm a convulsed peasant visited by the saint's *baraka* (blessing).

The *moussem* of Moulay Abdellah, in the neighbourhood of Al Shadida, that I saw later, enjoys different features because of its position, greater popularity and size. Situated by the sea, it turns into a huge Spanish-style fairground for a whole week. The large tents for dignitaries line up along the beach mixed up with those for the horsemen who've come from all over Morocco to participate in the equestrian exercises of the '*fantasia*'. Hundreds of smaller, more modest tents house whole families, bands of youths, holidaymakers and devotees of Moulay Abdellah. In the midst of the collective hubbub I identify a group of *buhala* from the brotherhood of Sidi Heddi – recognisable by their beards and ragged clothes – chanting litanies by the light of a candle. At dusk, when the heat wanes and the sea-breeze blows, an animated crowd fills the front, eager for amusement and novelty. It's not the raucous, noisy tumult of Hispanic cities: the outbursts are more measured and respect the nature of the festivity. In all, the atmosphere of freedom that reigns is in line with the general aspects of other *moussem:* women and girls walk round quietly at night, stop to chat to strangers, gratefully welcome courting and gallantry. Meetings, idylls, night-time rendezvous are sometimes agreed through signs and, protected by the holiness of the place, those sought after are not forced to justify their absences or account for their actions: the pilgrimage enables them to escape their usual reclusiveness and yet not infringe norms of modesty. The *moussem* is a fertile space of freedom where pilgrims forget the social pressures and alienation of modern life for a few days. The proximity of the sea and expanse of beach, and the ease of access to strangers affords adulterers of both sexes, lover-hunting wives and husband-seeking girls contact with likely candidates and the delights of an ephemeral adventure or promising idyll. According to a widespread popular belief, the *baraka* of the saint cloaks the activities of transgressors with a mantle of forgiveness and oblivion. A large number of Moroccan marabouts particularly encourage the desires of women: the *ziara* supports interchange and communication with the other sex in a propitious cultural framework. Moulay Brahim, for example, grants the grace of fertility and many women who visit the sanctuary alone return home fulfilled thanks to his miraculous virtues. This happy blend of licence and piety under saintly patronage shows at any rate how popular forms of therapy survive both in rural areas and in urban centres atomised by the steam-hammer of technological, industrial society: the continuous flow to Moulay Brahim of cars with Casablanca or Rabat number plates and, above all, of Moroccan workers who have emigrated to France, Belgium and Holland, is clear proof of the emergence of a counter-modernity vital to assuage the inner devastation they suffer.

The worship of the saints developed under Islam in a form similar to what happened in the Christian world. The abolition of polytheism created an infinite distance between the individual and his Creator facilitating the appearance of charismatic mediators, enjoying celestial powers, in the community of the faithful. The relatives and friends of Muhammad played this role in the Islamic world and the Muslim saints of later centuries were always careful to link themselves back to them through the *silsila* or chain of their 'initiation'. Veneration of these mediators dates back at least to the second dynasty of Caliphs: already in the fourth century of the Hegira numerous funeral monuments existed in Baghdad dedicated to the memory and worship of the *waliya* (the holy men).

The splendour and wealth of the Abbasid Caliphate – in complete contrast to the simple, pious life of the Prophet during his stay in Medina – aroused an ascetic-mystical reaction in Basra, where Rabiaa al Hadauia, the beloved of Pure Love lived, and in Kufa – the cradle of Sufism – that soon spread to Baghdad and the whole of the Islamic empire. The Sufis, as is well-known, internalise the Koranic revelation, reject a purely legalistic interpretation of the *sharia*, and relive, like Al Basthami or Ibn Arabi, the Prophet's night-time ascension to the heavens, scandalising sages and jurists alike. The spreading of their doctrines from the ninth century of the Christian era through the example and word of Nuri, Chibli and Hussein ibn Mansur al Hallaj, led to new, varied mystical currents, later expressed in brotherhoods like the Ottoman *malamatis* and *bektashis* of the fourteenth century. The first, for example, avoided any manifestation of piety and adopted outward behaviour calculated to bring upon them the *malama* or censure of their contemporaries: in this way, they tamed their pride, kept their piety secret, silently honed ideals of perfection. More radical still, the second scorned the practice of the 'pillars of Islam', except for the profession of faith: they drank wine, rejected any kind of conformity and chatted familiarly, even irreverently, with their divine Maker. When Ibn Arabi elaborates his doctrine of holiness, he very significantly places the *malamatis* in the higher category of the servants of Allah. The unbridled, rather extravagant behaviour of the so-called 'madmen of God' – from Nuri and Chibli to Sidi Abul Abbas, the patron saint of Marrakesh – was a powerful influence, as we shall see, in shaping popular Moroccan religiosity and the atavistic cult of hermits.

One insight into Ibn Arabi's theory deserves comment here. In his major work, *Revelations of Mecca*, the great mystic from Murcia establishes the existence of three concentric spheres, the first of which, *waliya* or holiness, contains the others: while God's messenger (*rasul*) is both prophet (*nabi*) and saint (*wali*) the prophets are only saints and wander exclusively in the circle of holiness never reaching the inner spheres. Mohammed was thus messenger, prophet and saint, but a saint isn't an envoy of God or a prophet. Together with his bold exposition of a doctrine the implications of which I cannot dwell on here, Ibn Arabi wrote a hagiographic compendium of saints that he met on his journeys, pilgrimages and wanderings, translated into Spanish by Asín Palacios with the title of *Vidas de santones andaluces*. One of the most revealing features of holiness conceived by our author is its extension to particular objects or privileged places. As Michel Chodkiewicz says, paraphrasing his ideas, earthly space is not neutral: 'the visit of a saint or his posthumous presence in some way configure a field of benign forces'. Just as there is a hierarchy of spiritual dwelling-places, so there is one for physical locations: cemeteries, hermitages and graves enjoy the immediacy of angels, little genies and holy men who rest or roam there.

If the orthodox reaction to Sufism judged its metaphysical speculation, lack of interest in the prescriptions of external law, wish to enter into direct, personal contact with the Divinity as harmful, the worship of saints defended by Ibn Arabi was also the object of severe criticism. The famous *hanbali* polemicist Ibn Taymiyya, author of the pamphlet entitled *Difference between God's Saints and Satan's Saints*, attacks the doctrine of intercession, the commemoration of *mouloud* or the birth of the Prophet, and visits to the tombs of ascetics and mystics. The influence of Ibn Taymiyya, particularly on the

Arabian peninsula, provoked the development of the Wahabbi movement and the consequent destruction in present-day Saudi Arabia of all tombs, holy places and hermitages venerated for centuries by Muslims. A hundred years later, similar efforts by the Salafia tried to destroy the worship of Moroccan saints and the abuses of maraboutism. The holy war waged by the Salafis against pilgrimages, 'plebeian' brotherhoods and trance-inducing ceremonies led to a head-on clash with deeply rooted popular and rural religious practices: their ideal of a severe, purified Islam was at odds with the spontaneous, pragmatic religiosity of the majority of their co-citizens. Condemned at once in the name of Islamic orthodoxy and the values of 'progress', the worship of saints has not only continued but has recently become a source of comfort for millions of believers, victims of underdevelopment and bruised and battered by cruel, unbridled modernity.

A European interested in popular Moroccan religiosity is confronted from the outset with a problem of terminology: while the words *salih* and *wali* – synonyms for saints used indiscriminately – circumscribe the kernel of its meaning, the term *mrabit* from which is derived marabout – defined in dictionaries (you may well laugh) as 'a Mohammedan hermit' – does not merely refer to the holy *merbut* or his hermitage: it likewise encompasses his corpse, holy place, tomb and even nearby crags and trees. In Morocco, there are several land-scapes that enjoy mysterious emanations of saintly strength: fountains, waterfalls, rocks, cemeteries. As Touceda Fontela points out in his work on the Heddaui, members of the brotherhood of Sidi Heddi consider that the fish in the river next to his *zawiya* are blessed and piously provide them with food. As in the rest of North Africa and in sub-Saharan Muslim countries, a range of seers, soothsayers and cartomancers attributes to itself the marabout's miraculous gifts and, for years, users of the Paris underground, particularly in stations in districts densely populated by Africans, have got used to the presence of people distributing propaganda for famous marabouts, able to supply their customers with services ranging from a coveted job and the eternal love of one's lover or mistress to the ruination and terminal expulsion of enemies from French territory. One hardly need add that this exploitation of ignorance, superstition and helplessness has little to do with the worship of marabouts by devote Muslim men and women.

The Moroccan countryside is dotted with white-domed hermitages, their sober simplicity conferring a subtle, peaceful serenity on the surrounding area. With a single brush stroke some whiten an austere panorama of prickly pears and thorny bushes; others crown the crest of a hill fanned by the leaves of a wild palm tree or rise up proudly above rocks and promontories, battered by the waves and impregnated with salty luminosity. Some are poor and dilapidated, as if the *salih* who lived there had over time lost the strength of his *baraka:* their walls fall into ruin and no pious soul lavishes care on them. Some, on the other hand, show off green tiles or crenellated balustrades or a shaft of metal at the centre of the dome, as in mosques, crossing three bronze balls the size of which diminishes from sphere to sphere or else sustaining a golden crescent moon its tips pointing skywards. The most popular, most frequented hermitages display the signs of the veneration they receive. As in other religions, the worship of intermediaries in Islam is not disinterested: the faithful seek favours and make pledges to that end. In order to leave a record of them and perhaps prompt the saint's memory, Moroccan devotees, male and female, hang clothing, knotted ribbons and similar garments on the *salih's* tomb, on his holy place, even on nearby trees and shrubs. This ancient tradition of pledges, practised by Cuban *santeros* and witches on the *ceibas* or sacred trees of the island, is widespread in North Africa, Egypt and Turkey: I remember how in the garden behind the wonderful mosque of

Suleyman in Istanbul, I discovered a tree festooned with hanging votive objects and ribbons. The seven patrons of Marrakesh – hence its name, the medina of the Seven Men *(sebaatu rxal)* – protect its inhabitants and particularly the brotherhoods dependent on their favours; along-side them, other saints in neighbouring districts like Sidi Rahhal, Sidi Yahya al Kartubi, Moulay Brahim or Buya Omar cure illnesses and people possessed by devils or endow women with the precious gift of fertility. The doctrine of Ibn Arabi confers, as we saw, the endorsement of *Chij al Akbar* (Supreme Master) on worship of those places and dwellings enriched by the presence or visitation of a *salih*.

As Louis Rinn and Dupont and Coppolani describe in their books on Muslim brotherhoods, holiness in popular Islam springs from two distinct sources, or *muhibb*, which are sometimes superimposed: the initiatory and the hereditary. The first derives its legitimacy from a spiritual mastery transmitted from generation to generation by a 'chain' of saints according to the norms of the Sufi brotherhoods: this *silsila* dates back in some to the prophet Mohammed and even to the archangel Gabriel. The second, widespread for centuries in rural areas, presupposes the transmission of the spiritual powers of the founder of a *zawiya* to one of his children or to the whole of his offspring. In his *Journeys*, Ali Bey evokes with humour and grace the life and deeds of Sidi Ali Benhammed and Sidi Alarbi Benmat – whose theocratic government encompassed entire regions emancipated from the authority of the Sultan – accompanied by a flock of poor people singing their praises and armed men ready to defend them with gunfire: 'I've already noted,' he writes, 'that the divine privilege of holiness rewards certain families: the father of Sidi Ali was a great saint; so is Sidi Ali and Sidi Bentzami, his elder son, is also well on the road.'

As in the Christian world, the hagiography of many saints confuses history and myth. Dermenghem mentions the case of Lella Mimuna, whose cult flourishes in different parts of Morocco: while one Lella Mimuna seems linked to the figure of the saint Abu Yaaza and his tomb, near hers, which are jointly visited on pilgrimages, another exists linked to Moulay Buselham whose sanctuary is in al Garb and even a third, revered in the valley of Taffert. Orthodox Islam clearly distinguishes between the genuine miracles of prophets (*muaaxizat*) and the prodigies attributed to the saints (*karamat*). The charismas and portents that halo saintly lives are judged to be secondary and even insignificant by the Sufis themselves. The lives of the great saints of Islam contain a wealth of anecdotes attesting to their contempt for supernatural gifts and powers. Fasting, poverty, mortification, humility are better preparations for the path that must lead them through the 'stations' of knowledge to the love of God and from there to a 'transforming union'. 'Gently tread the earth', says the Sufi, 'soon it will be your grave.' The lover of God (*muhibb*) or the one caught by divine love (*mexdub*) are indifferent to criticism and to praise, possess nothing and are not possessed by any desire, do not do good in the hope of rewards beyond the grave. Eight centuries before Gutiérrez de Cetina, author of the famous madrigal *Serene, clear eyes*, the Egyptian Dzuaal Nun said: 'if the Beloved doesn't look upon you with the eye of charity, he'll at least look at you in anger'. During the thirteenth century the influence of Sufi mysticism and the philosophy of Algaceli and Averroes enriched the spiritual life of the Maghreb. But the antiphilosophical and anti-esoteric reaction, first of the Almoravids and then of Al-Mansur, sealed the triumph of the theologians and their narrow legalism: deprived of their sources of refreshment, popular Sufism is transformed into spontaneous maraboutism and nourishes the petty kingdoms of the *zawiya*s.

The same vagueness in relation to the semantic field of 'marabout' surrounds the meaning of *zawiya*. The multiplicity of its functions, diverse origins, the deep differences between rural and urban *zawiya*, the one which protects the founder's remains and a centre affiliated to it, require clarification. In Marrakesh and the surrounding country-side, to give one example, it is difficult to find a common denominator for bourgeois *zawiyas* organised as neighbourhood religious associations and those in Sidi Rahhal or Buya Omar where a colourful, anachronistic court of miracles conjures up a medieval scenario. Basing himself on their different goals, modalities and sources of finance, Abdellah Laroui suggests a concise typology: '*Zawiya* – social centre in rural areas, where people shelter, convalesce, sort out quarrels, exchange products, are entertained: at once hotel, clinic, market, fair, court, school. *Zawiya* – urban club where one goes to rest and swop advice and news between working in the shop and returning home. *Zawiya* – monastery. *Zawiya* – hermitage, the historical proto-type of the others, either abiding by its original purity or blended with any of the preceding modalities. *Zawiya* – principality, able to expand and take in a province where the *sayyid* monopolise positions and enjoy total authority. *Zawiya* – order or brotherhood, that can be limited to a family, a clan or else can include as servants, adepts and employees a good section of a region's population.' The evolution of the Moroccan *zawiyas* is inextricably entwined with the historical vicissitudes of the power of the Moroccan royal dynasty. From their establishment as simple refuges for pilgrims and wandering Sufis to their transformation into principalities semi-independent of the sultan's authority, they play a pre-eminent role in the fragmented, complex society. When canonical, official Islam is unable to bind together the different components of the Moroccan social *corpus*, the brotherhoods linked to an 'initiated' chief proliferate and acquire a great impetus. Their originally private, esoteric nature in effect renews a spirituality made limp by legalistic routines and overwhelmed by the weight of formal religiosity.

The condemnation of power corrupted in the name of mystic values won many adepts and forced the monarchs to oppose their subversive action. As Mohammed Kably points out, the founding of some *zawiyas*, like the one in Fez, obeyed the need to 'disseminate official ideology and psychological action' to travellers. The struggle between both tendencies, the courtly and the popular, develop ineluctably throughout the fourteenth century: the theses of the first, sustained by Ibn Abbad of Ronda and Zarruk combat, as in more recent times, the superstition and rural backwardness of their adversaries who, busy 'like old ladies fussily seeing to their clothes, walking-stick, rosary and necklaces, they say, they ignore all prohibitions and surrender to every form of earthly pleasure.' From the time of the propagation of the marabout movement of Mohammed Shazuli, the *zawiyas* have always flourished at a time of weak central power: the real division of the country into *bled al mapjen*, under the authority of the Sultan and *bled siba*, dependent on local religious leaders. Even a summary account of the great *shorfa* of the sixteenth century to the present ruling dynasty – the birth of the *nasiria, charkauia, uezzania zawiyas* – would take too long. At any rate, the process generating the *zawiyas* is the result of the conjunction of local maraboutism and the initiatory esoterics of the brotherhoods: a point of convergence, which, Berque reminds us, clarifies its polyvalent character. Each new *zawiya* springs from a previous branch, like a rebellious, green shoot: its driving aim is to rejuvenate a weary tradition but gradually degenerates into mere management of property bequeathed by the founder and, sometimes, in a bloody struggle for succession and the privileges of the *baraka*.

The role of the *zawiya* in Morocco today has lost part of its importance; but its shedding of political pretensions hasn't erased its spiritual influence. Attacked by Salafism and present Islamist tendencies, it has transmuted its ancient function as a shelter against the abuses of despotism into a new form of shelter against the rootlessness and alienation created by modernity.

We who live in the old areas of Marrakesh often bump into a group of brothers playing their instruments in an alley or square, on their way to the *hadra* or weekly Friday meeting, a private party organised by a family to ingratiate itself with its patron saint or celebrate a lucky event. The brotherhood of the *hamadcha*, where I have some friends, exhibits its red embroidered green standards mounted on wooden poles topped by a copper ball like those decorating mosques: the *juan* or 'brothers' rhythmically beat their *daaduaa* which they rest on their left shoulders as they head leisurely towards their rendez-vous under the intrigued gaze of locals peering from their doorways. In the closed ceremony I attend, the session begins with a recital of Koranic chants and litanies by Sidi Ali Ben Hamduch, buried with his disciple Sidi Ahmed Dghughi in the mountain fastness of Zerhoun, not far from Meknes: it is the *ddker* or chant of a divine name which I shall refer to later. When the leader gives the sign, the younger brethren begin to dance in a circle, barefoot, arm in arm. Sometimes swinging to the right or the left, on one foot or the other, sometimes jumping in unison or beating the ground with the soles of their feet. In their weekly meeting, the hitting of instruments is obsessive, frantic: sometimes a musician collapses and enters a state of trance. But, ordinarily, they are well-controlled ceremonies where, unlike the big fiestas of the brotherhood – the Prophet's birthday, the pilgrimage of Moulay Idris el Zerhun – blood doesn't run.

Like the Shi'ite flagellants in the month of Moharram, commemorating the martyrdom of the imam Hussein or the penitents of Holy Week, heirs to the medieval gatherings of flagellators, the *hamadcha* seek to approach the Divinity through expiation and purification of the senses. The chant, dance and percussion of their instruments leads to that 'encounter' or psychic state when, with astonishing fearlessness, they beat their heads with small spiked maces or make cuts in their skulls with two-headed axes shaped like pikestaffs, possessed by an ecstasy of self-punishment beyond suffering or pain.

I have also occasionally attended the weekly meetings of the brotherhood of the *derkaua* in their *zawiya* near the Djemaa el Fna. The building housing it is at the end of an alley and the remains of some leaders and members of the order famed for their piety and lives lived apart rest in the peaceful inner garden. The *derkauas* have congregated in the room where they recite their prayers, seated on rush-mats, leaning their backs against the wall: the majority are mature in years and they are waiting for the master to arrive and initiate the oration. Their founder, Al Arbi al Derkaui, exercised great spiritual influence at the beginning of the last century and 'brothers' of the order were distinguished until recently by studded sticks, rosaries with heavy beads and green turbans. Today, they seem to have abandoned their wandering ways and some at least have accepted the servitudes of civilian life: artisans or owners of small shops, they practice an intense, monotonous *ddker*, either the profession of faith or another Koranic sentence, or the infinite repetition of God's name. After a while, the 'brothers' bow gently forward and back, chant the *La ilaha illa Allah* and suddenly rise up, like Konya dervishes, for the *aaimara*. When Dermenghem visited them they still sang the passionate esoteric poems of Ibn al Farid, the mystic dubbed the 'Sultan of the Beloved'. Today, they limit themselves to moving from the proclamation of divine Uniqueness to the gradual reduction of the Allah en Lah to Hua (He), Hu and even H, hoarse gasps, syllabic breaths, surging deep from within their chests. Their trance is neither convulsion nor paroxysm. After the ecstasy, those present settle back on their mats, recite calming prayers and bid farewell with an expression of inner peace.

Although there are many brotherhoods with a distinct character and following, it is the *gnauas* and *aisauas* who enjoy most popularity. Founded by Sidi Mohammed Benaisa, the Perfect Master, who successfully bent the will of the Sultan who had exiled him and died in Meknes five and a half centuries ago surrounded by popular enthusiasm, the latter spread rapidly from Morocco to the Middle East, assimilated the practices and customs of the *gnaua* slaves and now has thousands of devotees. Their ceremonies and rites have been described in detail by Lane in Egypt and René Brunel in the Maghreb. The *aisauas* used to wear a plait down the middle of their shaved skull, share with the *hamadcha* their aversion to the colour black during *mouloud* and, unlike the other brotherhoods, allow women to join their ranks. Their processions behind standards embroidered in gilt lettering always draw people anxious to gaze on their ecstatic dancing and violent gestures. Their musical instruments – kettle-drums, bendires, ghitas – gradually fuse with the recital of litanies and initiate the dance: a cadenced movement of feet, bowing and beating of the ground with bare soles. After concluding this preparatory phase, the 'brothers' hold each other by the hand or shoulder till they have traced a circle, repeat the divine name with an increasingly intense rhythm, transforming the articulation into a bellow: with half-closed eyes and faces dripping with sweat, they sway their heads violently, spin like tops, seem to confront each other as if impelled by opposed forces or else clump together, accelerating their movements to a state of exaltation. After the banning of the *frisa* in the time of the protectorate – the consumption of the blood of freshly sacrificed animals, the sprinkling of knee-breeches and garments in order to be impregnated with the *baraka* of Sidi Mohammed Benaisa – the rites seem to have been tamed. The dances of representation or possession, in which each *aisaua* imitates the movements of the animal he identifies with (a lion, panther, jackal, or camel) – the 'extraordinary leaps', actions to 'disembowel and gut entrails', gestures of 'being devoured' described by Brunel – are still practised, so I have been told, on the annual pilgrimage to the tomb of the founder, but I have not yet had the opportunity to witness them. Nonetheless, the *aisauas*, known throughout Morocco, like their brothers in the *hnaichia* sect, as snake charmers, should not be limited to this colourful, folkloric image. Their fakir games with boiling water, embers and glass are nourishing expedients adapted to their vocation as dervishes. Close in so many ways to the *gnaua*, they are distinguished from them by the fact that while the latter usually arouse trances in third parties, the *aisauas* provoke them in themselves: like the *hamadcha* they fall stunned, convulsed, possessed by the spirit of the saint or an evil genie.

Though they originate from mountains near Tangier, the *heddaua* of the brotherhood of Sidi Heddi frequently visit Marrakesh and neighbouring pilgrimage points. From their beards, grime and patched djellabas, the *heddauas*, also called *buhala*, seem to be linked with some of the Sufi *tarikas* famous for their carefree ways and extravagances. Ramón Touceda Fontela dedicated a very interesting study to their history and the customs and formation of their *zawiya*. After sympathetically describing their ideals of ascesis, kindness and help towards neighbours, their habit of collecting alms in souks by beating a drum and their return to the *zawiya* with shell-studded *zabala* full of victuals, he focuses critically on other aspects of their monastic life: if the *buhali* has to be single, divorced or a widower – any relationship with a woman involves immediate expulsion from the *zawiya* – he is on the other hand a relentless smoker of kef and keen on sodomy. These customs, about which they are quite open, bring them close to the figure of the *mexdub*, whose strange, eccentric behaviour is for devotees additional proof of saintliness. '*Buhali*', writes this author, 'means "fool", "madman", "weak-witted man", "a wretched butt of jokes". The *heddaua*, like "God's madmen", maintain an ideal of the austere, vagabond life, indifferent to the contempt their matted hair, appearance, beards, ragged clothes, dirt, bare feet arouses in rich, decent people. The last traces of a world that has almost vanished, their presence is nevertheless refreshing and invigorating: that grain of salt, as Dermenghem says of the Sufis, 'prevents intelligence from being corrupted and the norm being fossilised by routine'.

Cinema Eden

The brotherhood of the *gnauas*, mainly comprising descendants of slaves brought from Guinea or the Sudan, was founded by Moulay Abdelkader and its social origins and rites of initiation situate it at the antipodes of the aristocratic brotherhoods of Morocco. Their rites, as we shall see, are both therapeutic and religious. While the *gnauas* are usually known to tourists visiting Marrakesh from folkloric displays in the Djemaa el Fna, their group attracts a growing number of adepts and followers whose psychic problems, inimical to treatment by modern medicine and hospitals, discover traditional ways to a cure via the ceremony of the trance. Uprooted peasants, lone women, artisans transformed into civil servants or bank employees come to their meetings hoping to recover their psychic equilibrium or to integrate themselves in an atmosphere of dense, tangible fraternity. The brotherhood helps them, as Lapassade notes very perceptively, 'not to deny modernity but to coexist with it', by giving meaning to their alienating work, eliminating inner obstacles to the convulsed expression of their desires and aspirations.

In the first week of November I followed the Marrakesh brotherhoods on their annual pilgrimage to Moulay Brahim in order to participate in the festivities of *mouloud* and the nocturnal ceremonies of the trance.

In my essay on the dance of the whirling dervishes,* I refer to the theological disputes over the *sama* or Sufi spiritual harmony and mention the *Reinvigorating of the Religious Sciences* by Algaceli, whose dual authority as teacher and philosopher endorsed the legitimacy of the ceremony. In one chapter in this work, entitled 'Book on the Proper Use of Listening and Trance', the author confronts issues of great importance related to our discussion. Before considering it, we

* see page 95

48

should remember how the Sufis were the first people interested in regulating the purity of the ecstasy of initiates in the esoteric way: they warned against shouts, laments, fainting fits, the tearing of the habit unless these obeyed irresistible impulses; they considered it was a proof of immaturity to start to dance before the state of mystic plenitude was attained. The trance, according to Al Hallaj, should arise spontaneously, like a divine gift. For Ibn Arabi, the highest degree of perfection for a Sufi consisted in controlling his movements and surrendering to quiet, rapt ecstasy. This distrust or fear of rapture on the part of a great mystic, is not, as we know, exclusive to Islam. When Saint Teresa of Avila experiences these impulses, 'I feel so embarrassed' she writes, 'that I want to hide myself away. I really beg God to take this from me in public.'

A trance can be provoked by the chanting of Koranic verses, the reading of poems – Mawlana, Ibn al Farid – or the performance of singers and musicians, but Muslim authors are usually discrete on this last point. Although, as Gilbert Rouget reminds us, Arab singing tends to move and inflame its audience which is in turn brought up to give free rein to its emotions, treatises on the subject are few and spare in details and explanations. While a story concerning Al Farabi attributes to this philosopher the faculty of provoking laughter, tears or plunging into apparently mortal slumber those listening to his music, the best known work on the subject, *The Epistle on Music* by the so-called Brothers of Purity *(ijuan el saffia)*, though it certainly examines the curative, medical influence of the latter on the body and its illnesses, is really a treatise on musical astrology full of subtle digression and intriguing mysteries.

The general bibliography on trances is vast and I cannot dwell on it here: despite the cultural differences existing, for example, between Cuba and Morocco, manifestations of possession in both countries are astonishingly similar and the same can be said, if we focus exclusively on the latter, in relation to profane and religious trances, the *tarab* and the *hai*. The famous Moroccan musical group of the Nas al Ghiuan is also known as 'people of the *tarab*', and is capable of arousing trances in theatre stalls: it isn't by chance that one of their masters was in fact a *gnaua* master in Essaouira and left the brotherhood that inspired the ritual *sebda* to devote himself to the music of the *tarab*. Conversely, one of the members of the modest group of barbers from the Djemaa el Fna that performed in various Spanish cities returned to his *gnaua* origins and today plays in sessions of mystical-therapeutic trances in the autumnal cool of the nights of Moulay Brahim.

The arrival of the different brotherhoods with their leaders, 'brothers' and standards, and the hubbub of the pilgrims attracts to the sanctuary perched in the Atlas a heterogeneous multitude and reminiscences of the medieval mingle suddenly with a stunning eruption of modernity. Buses, lorries, cars try to find a way through the throng to find a parking spot on the mountain terraces. Men, women and children, devotees leaning on the saint's walking-sticks, rush from one group to another, attracted by the rattle of drums and the spectacle of the dances. The modest hostels and pensions near the *zawiya* are at bursting-point: visitors who cannot find refuge there are forced to wrap their burnouses round them and sleep out. As in Moulay Abdellah, girls circulate at night leisurely and naturally. The sacred area of Moulay Brahim is a space of freedom.

Faced with the impossible task of following the rites, prayers and dances of the brotherhoods gathered here with a minimal rigour, I prefer to meet up with my *gnaua* friends and witness the ceremony of the trance with them. Members of the small band gather by night on one of the stepped terraces on the hill by the village, next to a wall lit by a simple bulb. Seated on rush mats, the musicians beat their instruments, drink tea at their leisure, fill the censor with benjoin or musk. The public has made a circle round them and those who arrive first sit on the sloping ground, jostling together without distinction of sex or age. There are more women than men: old women, opulent *materfamilias*, graceful, beautiful young women. The *gnauas* of Moulay Brahim are not aroused by the *ddker* as in their private meetings as a brotherhood: they don't seek the 'encounter' for themselves, but provoke it in the women who have come to listen to them. Their religious invocations are purely formal and usually accompany the collection of alms after the *uaxeb*.

Some women listen to the music with their eyes closed, as if waiting for the right moment, in an apparent effort of concentration. The *memlukin* or possessed even form brotherhoods and stay together days, weeks and even whole months in the *zawiya* of Buya Omar. The *gnaua* therapy consists in taming the minor devils or, to use a language more geared to European perspectives, integrates manifestations of hysteria and psychosis in the ritual celebrations of worship. The rich expressive language of the ceremonies of the trance clearly distinguishes those possessed by a djinn from those possessed by the repetition of the divine name and music. The morbid states caused by all kinds of states of conflict – whether personal, family or social – find their resolution in paroxysm. The tension, release and subsequent melting away liberate the nervous energy that is normally repressed and the *mriaha* feels relaxed and calm, better prepared than before to coexist with the hidden roots of their unhappiness and alienation.

A young woman in her twenties, with long black hair, gets up from her mat by the musicians, enters the circle formed by the spectators outside herself, as if deep in inner contemplation. Her movements are initially gentle: she leans her head and body forward, crosses her arms behind her back, breathes in the aroma from the censor, waits for the tune that will unleash the mechanism of the trance. When she connects with that, her gestures become frenetic, she bends and brushes the ground with her hair and whips the dust with it: a companion is forced to hold her with her arms crossed behind her back to stop her from falling, another covers her hair with the yellow scarf of Lella Mira, one of the musicians brings over the censor and makes her smell the benjoin. The girl convulses, shrieks, kneels before the censor, crawls along, her face veiled by her hair and the scarf of Lella Mira. When the music finishes, she stays stretched on the floor, sweet, beyond herself, serene, with the luminous beauty of a woman after orgasm.

As I experienced in several consecutive sessions, women who go to meet the trance belong to different social strata and follow a variety of motivations; all wait for the tune or melody which creates the spark and wear on their heads the scarfs with the colours of the devils or genies possessing them: black for Sidi Mimoun, blue for Sidi Musa. One of them, who is clearly ill, shakes her legs and spindly arms, inhales the aroma from the censor as if it was ozone necessary to her state. Another wears the veil of Aicha Kandicha, the siren or feminine demon of popular Moroccan mythology who seduces solitary walkers in shady woods or on the banks of streams with swaying hips and generous breasts. Finally, a young woman, whose howls and convulsions impelled those present to hold her and piously cover her with a blanket, suddenly sat up smiling ingenuously, looking around her as if she couldn't remember what had happened. Minutes later I saw her running and flirting with a youth in the circle of spectators round another brotherhood.

The clearly voluntary character of the trance, ruled by the musical 'key' that arouses it and the symbolic wearing of scarves, compels one to question its sincerity. While some women have lived a healthy, liberating experience – the possibility of associating their anxiety and misfortune with a familiar religious-cultural grouping – others had simulated the *uaxed* as pure entertainment or exhibitionism. Sufis severely condemn mechanical exercises in mystical experience and denounce their flagrant hypocrisy. However, the adaptation of their esoteric doctrine to a popular, culturally hybrid religiosity seems to support Algaceli. In his *Book on the Proper Use of Listening and Trance*, the philosopher admits, against the opinion of his peers, both deliberate and simulated trances: in order to learn the psychic mechanisms that set them off, he says, the neophyte can start by simulating them. The criteria is no doubt debatable and does not mention possession by demons but it leads one to be indulgent towards the actresses of Moulay Ibrahim. Like their anguished or sick sisters, they have also sought the *baraka* of a saint to break out of their isolation and communicate with strangers, to find lovers or boyfriends, to relieve suffering and grief, to enjoy a festive, stimulating environment, to follow a form of therapy, to find themselves again, to find solace, to connect their energies to the religious, mystic values embodied in the marabouts whose slender, diminutive tombs or hermitages dapple the green or crags of the landscape in white.

On my return to Paris, as I write these pages, I bump into a Spanish friend in the street whom I've not seen for months. Although we are both in a hurry, we sit down for a few minutes in a café. After an exchange of pleasantries on our respective appearances, she tells me she's just broken up with her husband, the routine of work is getting her down, she feels depressed and, the final straw, her psychiatrist has gone on holiday, leaving her up against the odds. What must she do to emerge from this pit?

Her loneliness saddens me and, as I say goodbye, I regret not having the time to tell her all I have seen and timidly recommend a trip to Moulay Brahim.

Bibliography

Jacques Berque, *L'intérieur du Maghreb (XV–XX siècles)*, Paris, 1978

René Brunel, *Essai sur la Confrérie Religieuse des Aissaoua au Maroc*, Paris, 1926

Henri de Castries, 'Les sept patrons de Marrakech', rev. *Hesperis*, Rabat, 1924

Michel Chodkiewicz, *Le sceau des saints. Prophétie et sainteté dans la doctrine d'Ibn Arabi*, Paris, 1986

Depont et Coppolani, *Les confréries religieuses musulmanes*, Algiers, 1892

Emile Dermenghem, *Vie des saints musulmans*, Paris, 1981

—— *Le culte des saints dans l'Islam maghrebin*, Paris, 1954

J Herber, 'Les hamadcha et les Dghoughiyyin', rev. *Hesperis*, Rabat, 1923

Mohamed Kably, *Société, pouvoir et religion au Maroc à la fin du Moyen Age*, Paris, 1986

Georges Lapassade, 'Les gnaua d'Essaouira', rev. *L'Homme et la Société*, Paris, 1976

Abdellah Laroui, *Les origines sociales et culturelles du nationalisme marocain*, Paris, 1980

Louis Rinn, *Marabouts et Khouans*, Algiers, 1884

Gilbert Rouget, *La musique et la transe*, Paris 1980

Ramón Touceda Fontela, *Los Heddaua de Beni Aros y su extraño rito*, Tetuan, 1955

TURKEY

Gaudí in Cappadocia

A TRAVELLER FROM BARCELONA who, on the journey from Nevşehir to Ürgüp, branches left toward the Avçilar valley en route to the famous cave churches of Göreme and Zelve sets foot on a terrain whose breathtaking strangeness does not entirely efface a diffuse, persistent impression of familiarity. Past Üçhisar, as the zigzagging road hurtles downwards, he contemplates a fascinating panorama that recalls well-known images. The shapes and structures of the volcanic space seem subtly fashioned by the genius of a land-scape painter. Behind sculpted bluffs and strata, white sinusoidal breakers, corporeal masses of opaque, gigantic proportion, sun-scorched escarpments from a lunar wasteland, the valley where he lands suddenly confronts him with a daringly vertical composition, a concatenation of elements possessed of beautiful, oneiric plasticity: cylindrical towers with scaly, curvilinear tops, steeples cone-tipped or bristling with spikes, candles dripping crystallised eruptive rock, pillars with little fungiform hats, window boxes and hefty pro-jecting cornices. Dwarfed by the dimensions of the forest, the visitor gradually recognises motionless spinning tops, giant, rustic chimneys, megaliths in unusual equilibrium, natural flying buttresses, ramified or truncated columns. The diverse elements seem to fit together like the spine, bones and muscles of organic beings and the observer witnesses a kind of apotheosis of naturalist fiction or illusion in which distortion of volume, compensation by foreshortening, structural arborescence envelop him in an unreal, enchanted aura of *trompe l'oeil.* Weightless, entranced, thrust into memories of other times, other places, he will instinctively seek out in the strangeness and rigour of the scene parabolic armatures, vaults with *mudéjar* stalactites, lobular or labial shapes, leaf patterns, tracery, floral geometrical motifs, valves, petals. Could the rocks, hooded like a procession of petrified penitents, possibly be cupolas, lanterns or ventilation shafts made of glazed tiles, earthenware and shards? Imperceptibly, the distance from Cappadocia to Barcelona is wiped out: the miraculous space he treads leads inexorably to the auroral creation of Gaudí.

*　　*　　*

I first visited Cappadocia in 1979, a few weeks after the military coup which put an end to ailing Turkish democracy. The day after my arrival in Ürgüp the authorities embarked on a massive census of the population and forty million citizens had to stay at home: only the forces of order and census administrators had right of movement. When I wanted to leave my hotel, I was disagreeably surprised to find a guard with a bayonet in my way. Trapped with fifty odd Germans with whom I avoided all contact, I decided not to resign myself to their fate but to risk a foray out: I ran across the street ignoring the *ascari's* shouts and burst into the nearby police station. Loudly, I demanded my natural freedom, the tourist's inalienable right to move around and nose about. My anger proved to be persuasive since the duty-officer reluctantly granted me capricious entry to a totally depopulated area. For several hours, in the sole company of a friend with similar authorisation, I wandered through kilometers of desolate, eruptive landscape where I came across no living being except for insects, small birds, lizards and the dogs of a troglodyte, of whom more in a moment. In the empty diving-bell silence, the Cappadocia of volcanic stone, sculpted and forged by aeolian erosion, appeared to the two survivors spared by the cataclysm or atomic explosion with the evanescent beauty of a mirage.

A succession of tenacious memories and images: blessed calm of the universe after the Apocalypse; impression we were the last representatives of extinct *homo sapiens;* intense perception, through our five senses, of manifestations and signs of organic life after the catastrophe; a route across hillsides via tiny shortcuts, dubious tracks, paths leading nowhere which suddenly fade away. After the abrupt, austere plateau, the hallucinatory setting created by the combination of features brought me straight back to Gaudí: columns wearing caps or pointed hoods, lined up like alphabetising, emblematic pencils; forests of cones, needles, spires, obelisks; fossilised jellyfish; unexpected chromatic variations; disruption of normative functionalism; mystic incandescence; pure, rational architectonic delirium. In the Göreme valley and, beyond, on the way to Zelve, our gaze still embraced churches, bereft of the faithful, hollowed out of jagged escarpments or mounted in cones, abandoned monasteries, hermits' cells, walls decorated with painted or sculpted crosses, vestiges of the reclusive life of anchorites fleeing iconoclasts' fury, enormous cave hives complete with windows, passageways, stairs, lanterns, in which Christ, the Virgin and the Apostles alternate with St George and the dragon, St Catherine and St Barbara. Hellenic inscriptions, drawn by the monks, also recalled those which adorn monuments by Gaudí. In the course of that unreal, captivating ramble, as we climbed a somewhat uneven slope in search of a village, we were surprised by the bark, or rather chorus of barks, from a pack of dogs guarding one of the isolated grottoes or chapels. As we climbed, the ferocious barking intensified. Caution advised us to keep our distance but curiosity won the day. The path obviously led to an inhabited cave and, after a day wandering through a parched, deserted land, all fear was swept aside by our desire to communicate with someone else. When we reached the cave dwelling, we realised that we were not in danger: the dogs were well tied up and soon quietened down when their master cracked his whip. The troglodyte lived in a rectangular cave hollowed out a meter above ground level from the wall of the cavern which served as his porch: a chamber had been converted into a bedroom, with palliasse and pillows, and could be closed off from the rest by a half-drawn curtain. The fantastic layout of the place, its variegated decorations, enthralled me, and thanks to a snapshot I took I can describe them with some precision: a coloured portrait of Atatürk, religious prints, photographs of an old ramblers' club; sheepskins and cushions covered in brightly coloured material laid over the stone bench where the dogs slept. The owner with his white, sylvan beard was sitting on his bed reading and answered my greeting with a mere nod of the head. From time to time, ever absorbed in his reading, he would crack the whip to calm his anxious guards. I photographed the latter, stretched out on their sheepskins, and, before bidding farewell to my silent host, I surveyed the scene for the last time. It was then, while I inspected the small set made up of cavern and alcove, that I noticed a phrase scrawled in Catalan on the side cave: *Yesterday a master, today a shepherd.* Hadn't Gaudí written or said something similar?* At the risk of being called impertinent, I took a photo. But the film had got stuck or wasn't in properly: anyway, the photo never came out.

I left Turkey not knowing whether I had been dreaming or whether the graffiti really existed.

*   *   *

Back in Cappadocia six years later, my main objective is to find the old man. I can clearly remember my previous trek across the mountains and am sure I will easily locate him. Nevertheless, as I prepare to meet

---

* Gaudí's real phrase goes: *Ahir pastor, avui senyor*, in reference to the vicissitudes of his sleeping partner, the ennobled commoner, count Güell.

him, doubts besiege me. Will he still be shut away in the same spot? How will I manage to break his silence? With my hesitant, limited vocabulary, will I succeed in extracting from him what I want to know? What means should I use to open myself up to him and somehow win his confidence? As a precaution, to encourage our coming together, I decide to do without my camera. I shall visit him as an old friend, thanking him for his brief, chance hospitality. I am tempted by the idea of taking him a present but reject it: wouldn't this perhaps seem suspiciously like a clumsy attempt to buy his insights and knowledge? Better to appear calm and unworried, the opposite of that 'Greek bearing gifts' whose offerings, far from winning favour with the receiver, arouse his instinctive suspicion: I shall simply appear at the cave, unafraid of the ferocious dogs, as someone well-acquainted with the surroundings and the unquenchable personality of their master.

A taxi takes me close by; I immediately find my way between volcanic cones and rocks and within minutes am standing before the old man's home. A transistor radio is broadcasting Gregorian chants and I notice towels and clothes hung out to dry on the shrubs by the grotto. This time the dogs do not bark at me: they are dozing in the sun and look at me unconcerned. The old man is still resting on the palliasse in his bedroom, with the curtain drawn, in the same position as I had left him at the end of my previous visit: everything is exactly the same as before and it would seem natural for him to open our conversation with a softly spoken 'as we were saying yesterday . . . '

While I have recourse to my compendium of Turkish greetings and polite formulas, he is content to stroke the back of one of the dogs stretched out on the stone bench with the springy point of his whip. Rather embarrassed, I stand beneath the arched ceiling of the entrance to the grotto but he finally turns toward me and stares at me, questioningly.

'Are you Catalan?'

'No; I mean, yes.' His blue eyes look hard at me and I conclude: 'Well, not really.'

His mastery of the language has taken me by surprise. Cunningly, I contrive to hide this from him and refrain from asking how and when.

'The Master particularly avoids Catalans,' he points out. 'Nor does he want anything to do with Spaniards or foreigners who take interest in his work and write nonsense about it. But Catalans annoy him *most*.'

A long pause follows during which he looks me up and down as if to establish my true parametres.

'At least this time you haven't brought your Nikon,' he comments approvingly.

'Right, I preferred to leave it behind. I thought that . . . '

'You well know his phobia against photographers. Apart from the period when Audouart took a portrait and when the few snapshots were taken of him hiking with his father and niece, all photos were always taken furtively, taking advantage of some ceremony or deep religious devotion, as in the Corpus Christi procession in Barcelona. Do you remember?'

I say I do: I can see not the young red-haired architect, with his white complexion, gleaming eyes and light blue irises, high-bridged nose and lofty forehead, but an old white-haired, white-bearded man, candle in hand with a *canotier* under his arm, wearing a pair of rough shoes.

'With age, his phobia has got worse. If he discovers the presence of a camera-bearing tourist prowling around where he works, he immediately hides in the labyrinth of cave churches and doesn't emerge for some time.'

This new information, together with his continuous use of the present tense, leaves me literally confused: I listen without hearing as, mentally, I make a few basic calculations and review my unassailable truths.

'If I heard you right,' I finally declare, 'you're talking about him as if he were still alive.'

The old man nods in agreement and I ask, avoiding any hint of irony or humour: 'Has he been resurrected or do you believe in the transmigration of souls?'

'Neither,' he replies. 'He's still alive, that's all there is to it, and, what's more important, he's working night and day, like never before, putting the finishing touches to his immense work. Haven't you seen his latest chimneys and towers in the Göreme valley? They're the most perfect, consummate things he has ever created!'

'One moment,' I say. 'According to you, if I haven't forgotten the rules of arithmetic, he would now be approaching a hundred and thirty-four years of age, isn't that right?'

'What's odd about that? A drop in the ocean compared to the age of the old patriarchs in the Bible! Do I have to remind you that those holy men lived in these very mountains? Longevity is very common in these parts and you can meet very many centenarians in Cappadocia: most of them do not know their real age and they count it from the date that has been later added to their identity cards. As you well know, Gaudí comes from a family where many reach a ripe age. If his father lived to ninety-three in a city polluted by all kinds of moral and industrial waste, you can easily imagine what age he would have reached in these lands in which climate and frugality protect and preserve.'

My interlocutor throws a few crumbs to the dogs and uses my silence to scrutinise me again, apparently encouraged by my expression of sudden incredulity. The historical evidence which I can set against his arguments is considerable: the Number 30 tram which knocked Gaudí down on 7 June 1926, at the point where Bailén crosses Granvía; the reprehensible behaviour of the three taxi drivers who refused to drive him because of his threadbare clothes; the action of the Civil Guard Ramón Pérez, who took him to the Red Cross point from which he was moved to the Santa Cruz hospital; his famous, symbolic death agony amidst the poor in keeping with his pious wishes . . .

'Legends, just legends, the fruit of collective guilt and remorse! Uplifting scenes for the official hagiography!'

Unimpressed by his firmness of tone, I immediately bring fresh testimony to counter his undaunted delusions: the numerous shots of the funeral cortège as it passed through the Plaza de Cataluña, the Ramblas, the Calle Fernando, the cathedral. I can even remember the photographer's name, Segarra, and the presence of the photos in the archives of the Gaudí Chair. As the old man seems unshakable in his certainty, *de guerre lasse*, I have recourse to the supreme truth.

'Who, then, did they bury in the crypt of the Sagrada Familia, in the chapel of the Virgin of Carmel?'

The old man lowers his eyes for a few moments and when he meets my gaze again, he just asks quietly:

'Do you really think that the corpse of Santiago the Apostle is in his tomb at Compostela?'

*   *   *

Following the old man's written directions, you visit the fungiform cones and chimneys where, according to him, the Master has recently been at work. Although convinced he will dodge out of your way, will avoid your indiscreet presence nearby, you bring neither camera, exercise book nor sheet of paper to take notes: his misanthropy might have hardened, he tells you, and led him to hide away in the labyrinth of caves until you depart. Dressed in ochre, the colour of the ground you tread, trying to melt chameleon-like into the background, you reach the spot marked on the map. The striking unity of composition of the pawns, castles and bishops on the chessboard spread out in the valley transports you to a vision of the domes, chimneys and stairwells of Can Milà. Stony plinths, whose relief and ridges emphasise the use of mortar stones and the natural prisms of basalt, cross the uneven terrain between the rocky cones and you excitedly discover the hidden presence of home-made bricks and glazed shards. As with the Pedrera or Güell Park, the spectator witnesses a gradual symbiosis of the different structures in the landscape: ceramic materials, carefully adapted to local topography, are gently articulated into the sinusoidal swell of the nearby slope and the clear blue of the sky. The rough masonry of projecting stones is softened, as is Gaudí's wont, by the introduction of decorative elements and the organic naturalness of his finishing touches: seashells, tiny carved polychrome birds, nests of *trencadís* or shards. You can testify with your own eyes how the invisible hand of the architect has polished and refined the prodigious creation of the four elements: in the massive spinning top precisely marked by the old man, you find carefully laid out a subtle combination of earthenware, rows of bricks and fragments of tiles. When you penetrate the grotto cut out of the inside of the cone, you are suddenly right in Gaudí's ideal space: the light filters through cylindrical sky-lights, trapezoidal openings, and the staircase built centuries ago by the monks clings to the snaking line of the wall, twists in a spiral until it comes out on a kind of vantage point set on natural parabolic arches, cunningly concealed by an exterior granite parapet. You have hardly reached the top when you notice various signs of human existence: a small hearth made from lumps of stone, a rustic earthen-ware pot at the bottom of which are the by-now-dry remains of a brew of herbs, half-made plates and utensils. Their owner has recently abandoned the spot, perhaps rather hurriedly, since in his flight he left behind the bag where he was collecting proof of his fondness for mycology and botany. Could he have put his ear to the ground Indian-like and foretold your intrusion into the enchanted forest? The Catalan graffiti scrawled on the glazed coping stone in the wall fills you with delight: *De la llar al foc, visca el foc de*

l'amor.* Your intuition leads you to examine the variegated manufacture of the wall in search of a possible message and you hit the
bull's-eye. Who on earth could have written that except Gaudí
himself?

On subsequent days, while painstakingly inspecting cones and
megaliths or snooping around the cave churches of Göreme, you
gather together fresh, irrefutable signs of his elusive immediacy: fires,
bunches of wild herbs, combs and utensils, created by his own hands.
As well as his renowned sayings: *La Glòria es la llum, Oh, l'ombra de
l'estiu.*† Sometimes, like a wily, scheming genie, the Evasive One takes
a jesting pleasure in changing the content of his message: *Al cel tots en
serem d'actionistes.*‡ One evening as you trawl the warren of troglodyte
dwellings in Avcilar, he will slip through your hands by only a few
minutes: the pot where he boils his herbs is still steaming. You wait all
night, but he does not appear. Resigned, you crouch by the fireside
and slowly sip the infusion prepared by the Master with the absorbed
devotion of someone about to take communion.

*   *   *

Settled in his bedroom hewn from the rock, the old man wraps
himself round with his sheepskin coat and woollen blankets,
apparently chilly despite the heat. The dogs seem sunk deep in
lethargy and remain, during your conversation, on the lower bench
covered in sheepskins, as if poisoned or drugged.

'What you have already seen and many other things that you will
discover as you extend your knowledge of the area are the logical
culmination of a process that has been gestating for years. Had he not

---

* From the hearth to the fire, long live the fire of love.
† The Glory is the light, Oh, the shadow of summer.
‡ In heaven we'll all be shareholders. In fact, after listening to Clavé's choirs, he
   commented: *Al cel tots en serem d'orfeonistes* – In heaven we'll all be choristers.

once said that to follow nature is a way of continuing divine creation? Originality, he insisted, is the return to origins. His interest in Fra Guerau's rocks and the Prades mountains, his membership of the Catalan Association for Scientific Excursions were a response not only to his passion for geology and botany, they were also a reflection of an inner need fired by mystic longing. His previous work, subject to the whims of his so-called patrons, seemed botched beside the creative possibilities offered by the landscape. Thus, rather than abstractly reinventing existing forms, he proposed to enrich and enhance the gift-offering of nature. Eroded slopes, cliffs and rocks follow the same norms that rule the domain of architecture. What is the difference between the rocky cliff of the Pedrera, a truly urban mountain, and those one can observe here? So what if the volume and tortuous shapes of that huge stone forest in Avçilar are a product of tectonic activity, aeolian erosion or have been elaborated by the Master? In any case, don't they respect the laws of balance and gravity? The futile waiting and humiliations of his last years in Barcelona, unable to advance the works of the expiatory temple of the Sagrada Familia, filled him with bitterness and he instinctively sought out happiness and light. Here, in his hermit's retreat, he was able to carry through his old naturalist ruminations: instead of purely geometric and func-tional structures, his are geological and even organic. His work is a humble extension of Creation!'

The old man breaks off his speech to light a fire. You don't dare to guess his age, but since your first meeting his health has gone down-hill. As he gets out of his alcove you notice how he shivers from cold and seems to suffer from slight trembling fits. For a few moments he looks through the bedroom shelves and takes out a metal saucepan half-filled with water, into which he places a handful of herbs.

'But why did it have to be Cappadocia?' I ask at last.

'Gaudí was always attracted by the ascetic life of hermits,' the old man replies. 'In his cell in Güell Park, perhaps you already know, he slept on a straw mattress and once, I think in 1894, nearly died as a result of rigorously fasting during Lent. There could be nothing more natural for him than to disappear from that mediocre, positivistic world which was stifling him, to take refuge in the land where the first monasteries and communities of monks were founded. Like the Aramaic and Chaldean refugees from persecutions and massacres, he would find his ideal habitat in the life of a troglodyte, in these magnificent cave churches.'

'Of course, I agree, it's a seductive explanation; but it does not solve the riddle of his reappearance in these parts. I can see nothing in the public period of his life – if indeed our version of the facts is correct and he is still living and working here – to establish any kind of link between him and Cappadocia. Did he perhaps know the area from some engraving or photograph? Is there any evidence or proof that he ever referred to it?'

'Do you think he might have simply come in search of the mysterious 'Satalia' described in *L'Atlàntida* and that old Mossèn Jacinto Verdaguer locates in Asia Minor?'

'I must admit I had never thought of that. But it's still only hypothesis.'

'Look, young man – because that's what you are to me though you're fifty-odd – he was fascinated by the physical and cultural space of Islam. The only journey of his youth outside Spain was not to Paris, not even Italy, but to Morocco. In the archives of the School of Architecture in Barcelona where he studied there were photographs of Hindu temples and minarets in Cairo. He was equally very attracted by the slender minarets of the Sahara and the Sudan. He was never inspired by the Renaissance nor by neo-Classicism: like Cervantes and Goya, he sought out real Spain, which he found in the hidden strata of meaty *mudéjar* miscegenation. His absolute rejection of the system and criteria of his time led him to affirm his own values in the face of those which enjoyed universal respect. His apprenticeship in solitude was hard but fruitful. As he gained confidence in his own truth, he rejected and distanced himself from the truth of fellow countrymen. Bourgeois *bon seny* and *avara povertà* (common sense and grasping poverty) clashed with the white heat of his mystic ardour. Gradually his youthful *mudéjarismo* assimilated the Gothic and the Baroque, opened out in an unbounded vision of the exuberant geometry of nature. Man must rise up constantly, day by day, because inspiration is not enough. Europe could no longer bring anything to him: that is why he came here.'

'This is all very plausible,' I reply. 'However, historians require proof and, apart from a series of fairly alarming assumptions, the fact is we haven't any. If I am not mistaken, in the crypt of the chapel where his tomb lies . . . '

'Don't talk to me about memorial stones or plaques! I only have to read 'So-and-so was born, lived and died here' for the unbridgeable gap between reality and the written word to fill me with doubts. Who will guarantee that that is true? Couldn't they be made-up facts, details to strengthen the supposedly historical narrative and the laws of verisimilitude? Remember Herodotus and Vives' lapidary phrase: *Mendaciorum pater!* If all biographies are fictions, why should Gaudí's be true? Many, many years ago I read the only really convincing inscription on a beautiful timbered mansion in the French quarter of New Orleans: 'Napoleon was invited to live in this house after his defeat in Waterloo.' Finally I had found some incontrovertible evidence! He was invited, he was certainly invited: *but he did not go.*'

'So, according to you . . . '

'Stop piling up dubious evidence and surrender to the understanding in your heart! Gaudí withdrew from the world like a novitiate in a closed order after proclaiming his vows and, in a solitary state, impervious to criticism and praise alike, he continues his masterwork. The panorama you can contemplate in Cappadocia reveals the apotheosis of his genius. Patiently, humbly, you can follow alone in the steps of his mystic, creative itinerary. But you must be spiritually prepared for that encounter and deserve it; in a word, become worthy of him.'

The old man finishes boiling his infusion and pours the contents of the saucepan into two earthenware bowls. It is a bitter brew: it tastes curiously similar to the one prepared by the invisible troglodyte in the underground labyrinths of Avçilar. As on that occasion, my senses seem to be sharpened as I drink, and I am simultaneously filled with a pleasant feeling of peace.

The flickering, changing flames of the fire swathe in light and darkness the still bodies of the three dogs, stiffened by *rigor mortis*.

*　　　*　　　*

In order to be purified and to distil your senses and ideas, you begin by getting rid of your possessions and selfish utilitarian criteria: you sell your camera for a derisory sum which you hand over to a beggar crouching by the entrance to the mosque; you pay your hotel bill and divide your belongings between porters and waiters; poorly dressed, like the architect on the day of his accident, you leave the comfort of Ürgüp and head with a small bundle to the cones and chimneys of the sun-scorched splendour of Avçilar. Your presence there is to be light, discreet, wandering like the Master's. You learn to find shelter in the abandoned caves and churches, to sleep on an empty stomach, do without a watch, feed on infusions of dried herbs, savour the diaphanous fullness of the landscape, refine and polish day after day your understanding and sensibility. Elusive and attentive, inaccessible and near, Gaudí watches over your movements and from time to time reveals to you his kind concern: in the chapel of a cave monastery whose columns with their parabolic arches support an architrave decorated with round medallions identical to those in Güell Park, you find a page bearing Verdaguer's verses on the garden of the Hesperides; at the top of one of the cones, perforated with cells and skylights like a gigantic beehive, when you come across graffiti of a quotation from Góngora – *All is strange, the design, the manufacture and the means* – you are unsure whether it refers to his singular creative venture or to the sumptuous delirium of Cappadocia. Sometimes, when you take shelter in the shade of some cavern, you discover ready, steaming, especially prepared for you, the saucepan or pot in which he usually prepares his brews: thirsty, gasping, you cautiously sip the infusion, noticing immediately how your body becomes subtle and light beyond the restrictions of time and space: a stroll begun amid the fungiform columns and motionless spinning tops of Zelve extends unbroken to the flat roof and mosaic adornments of the Pedrera or the paths flanked with garden-boxes in Güell Park. Artifice and creation fuse; the apparent chaos of the landscape emphasises in fact the subtle harmonising of its features, the secret hand of the dragoman. By night, the physical volumes and shapes come alive, the silhouettes of the hooded cones lengthen and you witness from your burrow a solemn procession of penitents, between megaliths and torches, en route to the steep slope of his urban mountain, to the balanced verticality of the towers of his Temple.

Despite the repeated instances of tact and friendliness, Gaudí avoids any meeting. After downing his pleasant herb infusion, you shout in vain at the top of your voice that you have nothing to do with the Calvets, Batllós, Milàs from your contemptible country, that you hate as much as he the rapacious bourgeoisie which used him without understanding him, that you too have broken free and roam stateless through the places and lands that fascinate him; yet your voice is lost in the valleys corroded by aeolian erosion, down cracks and crevices in stones subjected to slow, millenary torture. The day you at last think you spot him, struck in a kind of cameo, pale, red-haired, bearded, straight-nosed, open-featured, as in Audouard's photograph, you realise your eyes are closed and you are daydreaming. In spite of your regular consumption of herbs with hallucinogenic qualities, the miracle or vision does not take place.

*   *   *

In the course of the weeks of my frustrated siege of Gaudí, I threw overboard a number of habits, I denied myself and fasted, mortified the senses, dwelt in a tranquil present, swore a temporary vow of poverty, lost several kilos, aged with a greyish beard, embraced my hermit's condition elated yet stern. The awaited adventure escaped me but I was consumed by the ardour of the chase.

Weak and despondent, I abandoned the Gaudian universe of Avçilar and Göreme and, before returning to my departure point, I went to bid farewell to the old man. An obsessive, despotic sun charred the long-suffering stone landscape and even lizards and insects seemed to be in hiding. A few meters from the cavern, I was surprised by the palpable density of the silence. Nobody was there and the interior of the room – bench, alcove, shelves – looked desolate and looted. The few belongings and pieces of furniture had vanished with their master and someone had angrily burnt the last traces of his presence.

*   *   *

The herbs used in the infusions and brews that I drank during the period spanned by the narrative and my writing grow wild in the mountain areas of the Mediterranean basin in Anatolia and in Catalonia. Gaudí used to look for them on his frequent trips into the hills but never revealed the recipe for their preparation. If he died, as official history claims, he took his secret with him to the grave.

The Palimpsest City

A Polyglot Discourse

IN HIS THOUGHTFUL ANALYSIS of the *Semiotics of a City*, the distinguished linguist Juri Lotman, founder of the Tartu School, observed that the city, 'as a complex semiotic mechanism and generator of culture, can fulfil its mission to the extent that it embodies a fusion of heterogeneous texts and codes, belonging to different languages and levels (...) The architecture, rites and ceremonies of the metropolis, its layout, the names of its streets and thousands of other vestiges of past epochs appear as coded programmes allowing the texts of its history to be constantly produced. The city is a mechanism that perpetually reproduces its own past, and is thus able to confront the present almost synchronically. From this perspective, the city, like culture itself, is a mechanism that opposes time'.*

The juxtaposition of layers of history and ethnicity in the metropolis necessarily encourages the existence and proliferation of collisions in time and space, the phenomena of hybridisation and dynamic mixing of discourses which in my view represent the unmistakeable stamp of modernity. The plurality and mingling of styles, reciprocal contagion, the energising value of osmosis decentre the gaze of visitors, obliterate their homogeneous vision of things, relativise and fracture initial global impressions. In the privileged streets and areas of the palimpsest space that is Istanbul, new arrivals stand and listen to a polyglot text, a babel

1 *Lettre internationale*, no. 13, June 1976.

of languages, the language of the stones, tracing the unwritten history of the city founded twenty-seven centuries ago according to the promptings of an oracle: Byzantium-Constantinople which, protected by the gods before devoting itself to the Christian Trinity and raising its slender minarets to the glory of the One and Only, overwhelms us both with the extraordinary setting and splendour of its monuments and the semiotic richness, its subtle interplay of synchrony and diachrony.

Urban Woods

Determined to domesticate the space of the big city, a newcomer strives with the help of guides and maps to establish a vision of the whole, scattered with reference points to ensure a quick path through the scabrous contours of its topography. Expert map-readers do not find this a demanding operation and it creates the illusory apprehension of a reality as simple and artful as the emergency supplies chest of the perfect tourist. This first investigative phase, imposed by our instinctive need to span, however superficially, the area of the unknown, yields to one where I believe fertile exploration begins: the overall vision fragments into a series of separate sequences, discontinuous spaces. Gradual acquaintance with objects upsets momentary certainties, fissures them like an earthquake: out of the city described in guidebooks, reproduced on maps, registered step by step by a traveller passing proprietorially through, arise isolated, apparently entirely disconnected territories, charged with a dramatic tension that hypnotises and subjugates.

Only the superficial observer of otherness can allow himself the luxury of the trivial themes of consumerism: the more familiar he becomes with the world he is penetrating the more difficult it will be to construct a plausible, straightforward image. Trawled district by district, street by street in my compulsive, relentless burning of shoe-leather Istanbul today appears on my mental horizon like a collage of postcards or a variegated patchwork whose only subject or linking thread will be the random pull of my meandering. Disoriented, decentred, *atypical*, I surrender myself to the stereophonic diversity of its codes, the dense foliage nourishing its history and thirst for life. I can't see the wood for the branches! It has been a long, enriching process. 'Wandering off a city's beaten track, like wandering off in a wood,' said Walter Benjamin, 'requires a whole separate education.'

Re-reading the City-text

On my first visit to Istanbul, some twenty years ago, what most caught my attention and immediately attracted me was the prodigious impression or air of animal strength: a savage, omnivorous, uncontrollable vitality overwhelming the traveller as soon as he steps foot there; the chaotic frenzy of the ant-hill – ants subject to the enigmatic determinations of destiny – which I have only found in one other metropolis that is both imperial and third-world: the bastard, migrant New York of black and Puerto Rican ghettos which are gradually spilling over and staining the white polity, a gentle contamination.*

In Istanbul, as in New York, the fight to survive shows itself by the light of day in all its calm, provocative brutality. The harsh need to earn a living, to survive come what may the onslaughts of an apparently insoluble general crisis translates into an excess of energy conferring on the slightest movement or gesture a sense of sudden determination, an internal tension which seem at first sight out of proportion. Instead of resigning themselves to their fate, the inhabitants react with a healthy impetuosity. The universal application of the

* See J. Goytisolo, 'Living in Turkey', *El País Weekly*, February 1980.

law of the fittest often forces them to be spare with feelings and adapt to a competitive, hostile atmosphere which forgives no frailty or error. A foreigner sometimes feels ignored, almost transparent. Looks seem to go through him, to aim at an object situated behind him. This non-existence, beyond the simple exchange of services, nevertheless has numerous advantages. A visitor becomes a film camera recording, in the minutest detail, the extraordinary microcosmos around him: buses, pedestrians, taxis, carts inventing impossible paths, fight to cut a route through all manner of obstacle, obey a set of improvised rules whose coherence and secret rhythm – like the almost fusional immediacy hidden in the hearts of the throng – he will not lay bare for months if not years.

The Pedestrian Mass

I am in the Eminönü neighbourhood where I usually linger in order to contemplate the fascinating spectacle of the crowd in motion: a cityscape as familiar to me by now as Turkish, no longer that language which struck the alert ear of Borges *as a softer form of German* and now a fortress patiently scaled and conquered. I can now speak to taxi drivers or traders in the Great Bazaar, but the impact of that first impression retains its vigour, intact despite the passage of time. If meanwhile my perception of the city has cracked like a broken mirror and my present haunts sit side by side with no linking theme, isn't the crowd's excess energy the inner magnet pulling my wandering steps through these physical and textual spaces that have irresistibly attracted me since I was a child? As with Tangier's Zoco Chico or Marrakesh's Djemaa el Fna, being there stimulates, bears fruit: life is transformed into a kind of collective writing exercise I discretely engage in without renouncing the delights of leisure.

From the quays of Üsküdar, the Bosphorus and the Marmara Sea, hundreds of thousands of commuters daily rush to attack the buses, invade the pedestrian-packed streets, swarm over the lifting-bridge joining the two sections of the city: a brusque popular army, hurrying, voraciously consuming *maashun* and sweetcorn, elbowing, propelling its way forward, as in metro walkways at rush hour. Leaning back on the rail, at the top of a pedestrian crossing, I eagerly examine the tide of faces climbing up the steps, the torsos and legs gradually emerging as their owners approach, reach, then leave me behind and walk down the other side, disappear from my field of vision. The expressive faces, lively gestures and mannerisms are a continuous source of wonder and solace. The contrast with the dead, lethargic, almost bovine visages that so abound in the cities of our industrialised North could not be sharper. As in my favourite areas of New York, with an imaginary camera, I never-endingly take snapshots of faces, silhouettes, gestures, looks. I only have to walk down to the waterfront or the environs of the New Mosque to be plunged immediately into a universe in perpetual motion: the ceaseless chatter of traders, water-sellers or porters bent double under their loads, versatile dealers in caps, scarves, bread rolls, lottery tickets. Almost everybody chews or masticates while leaping, running the distance to the ferries, buses, collective taxis which will take them to their destination.

I am in one of the most beautiful places that I know and, rather than describe the panorama from the Karaköy Bridge – the graceful lines of the Ottoman mosques, the golden rays of dusk on the tower of Galata, the boats manoeuvring to moor and depart the quaysides on either shore – my attention focuses on the wild, rustic face of a ferocious devourer of sandwiches swaggering piratically towards me on the arm of a friend. My snapshot has caught his inquisitive grimace and roughly sketched smile as he looked at me, flattered.

Cinema Eden

Self-Critical Interlude

Grasping your *Guide Bleu*, you could describe circumstantially to your readers the labyrinth of rooms structuring the harem of Topkapi Sarayi or wax expansively on the disposition of porticos, domes and minarets in Suleyman the Magnificent's mosque, a masterpiece, together with the Selemiye of Edirne, of the architectural genius of Sinan; you could embark *en route* with one of the noisy groups of tourists zigzagging between the admirable seascapes of the Bosphorus or visiting the islands of the Princes and their delightful entourage of sleepy Ottoman villas; could linger to contemplate the Byzantine walls or vestiges of the old hippodrome and thus enjoy, and help others enjoy, the rich profusion of the city's codes, its intricate polyglot semiology, but maniacal obsessive that you are, as alert as Baudelaire ever was to the urban hum, you prefer to climb the steep slope of Galipdede alone – leaving till later the review of its nearby monuments – and continue along Istiklal Caddesi before emerging on the left into the noisy, vulgar Passage of Flowers.

(You instinctively follow the crowd, heading into the most confused, densely populated areas and are blessed with the discovery, having just set foot in Istanbul, of the teeming district of *genel evler* or flat-roofed houses: you had crossed the bridge for the first time in your life and reaching the crossroads at Karaköy, on the way to Galata, were swept along by the throng into a side street protected by a frontier barrier, a guard post and two *ascaris*; but the somewhat oneiric account of your foray into the brothels doesn't fit here and the eager reader will find it in one of your novels. The price of an entry token at the time was a hundred non-devalued Turkish lira.)

The Passage of Flowers

The Çiçek Pasaji – as they now dub what in its heyday must have been one of the best covered walkways in Constantinople's cosmopolitan quarter – still displays the sign *Cité de Pera* on the front of one of its doors, the sign anachronistically evoking glories of old. The messages received by the spectator in the middle of a street lined by cheap eateries, vegetable, fruit and flower-stalls, emphasises the impression of exoticism and resigned acceptance of decline. A Frenchified bourgeoisie that once frequented the place vanished sixty years ago and its present clientèle recalls the one which populated the calle de Escudillers and Plaza Real in Barcelona when, as a university student, I walked down the Ramblas in search of a different atmosphere – one at any rate more suited to my interests and tastes – than the one I found at home.

L-shaped, its buildings seem to have suffered the consequences of a cataclysm or the general ruination of their owners before losing the glass canopy that once sheltered them, and exhibiting their present, dirty, down-at-heel state. While the nocturnal bustle mercifully hides the vista of crumbling walls and gutted rooms, a daytime stroll exposes the melancholy traces of old age. But the passage cheers up at dusk and tarted up by cheap jewellery and make-up, comes into its own like an astute old actress in the glow from the theatre footlights.*

The reduced space afforded by the area forces bar and restaurant owners to make the most of every corner, thus favouring chit-chat and enjoyable promiscuity. Solitary or paired off customers are immediately settled into the gaps between happy bands of drinkers with whom it is impossible not to fraternise. A language of signs soon incorporates the foreigner with no knowledge of Turkish into the

---

* The passage has been fussily refurbished in the hope of 'improving' the clientèle.

nuclear cell of some group, invited to share for minutes or hours the cordial, exuberant atmosphere. The hubbub which reigns requires of the foreigner a good ear to distinguish different species of voices and cries: the noisy conversation of friends, solemn toasts, orders shrieked by waiters into kitchens, scratchy tunes from a wan and weary combo, the patter of peanut and croqueted mussel vendors, numbers hawked by lottery-ticket sellers with their caps and Milli Piyango headbands.

Discontinuity, effervescence, immediacy, the coming and going of new customers, quarrelsome drunkards, momentary conniving, festive complicities. Some characters and players, repeated over the years, add a note of stability to the impetuous maelstrom of the throng: the malign, hunchback owner of one eatery, a seller of giant prawns who apparently windscreen-wipes the sweat from his face with his handlebar moustache, a stout, bespectacled, accordion-playing songstress who switches to a lively pasadoble on seeing me. Movements caught in flight: pieces of melon on forks offered to a neighbouring mouth, the mutual affection of two strapping youths feeding each other while continuing to tell their rosary beads. The space gives the impression of expanding to welcome new groups of visitors anxious for hustle and bustle. When the concentration of humanity goes beyond the limits of the unthinkable and one might think a pin wouldn't fit in, boundless Turkish fantasy is quick to give the lie: an acrobat installs his folding table in the very centre of the flux, places a stool on top, airily performs his tricks, a mocking, twin challenge to the physical capacity of the Çiçek Pasaji and the law of universal gravity.

The Great Bazaar

There is still time to mend your ways and exact a tardy if disgruntled pardon from your reader! Rather than dragging him along with you ecstatically to contemplate the pedestrian mass on a bridge and the rather cheap, tawdry spectacle of young *raki* drinkers, you can still take them, directed by the *Guide Bleu*, to places of finer vintage: to the Byzantine apse, narthex and mosaics of Santa Sophia; the imposing Valens aqueduct; the ruins of the Edirne gate through which Mehmet Fatih's infantry burst on 29 May 1453. Your wandering through the alleyways stuffed with wares and artisanry on the way to the Bayazit tower and Nuruosmaniye Camii raises the hopes of those anxious to get some hard facts on the city's palimpsest history: but here you are, not bothering to draw their attention to the splendid monuments nearby or to reciting guide-like the list of emperors and sultans (at least as many as Leon's and Castile's), you take the steep slope of Tarakçilar Sokaki and slip cool as a cucumber into the Great Bazaar!

Like a flash group of Madrid town councillors will you rush to haggle and then buy incredibly low-priced leather jackets and blousons? Your experienced advice to fellow countrymen fond of travelling to buy on the cheap would be extremely useful if one really deplorable fact didn't get intrude, that in like cases you always leaned the other way, outrageously favouring local sellers: using your knowledge of the vernacular to point out from afar, as in Marrakesh, the director of a big bank or an all-powerful ex-minister, indicating to shop assistants that they were well-heeled customers, that the screws should be tightened, no discounts allowed. In such an ornery frame of mind, your advice to your readers (whether councillors or not) would be counter-productive and, letting yourself be carried away once more by your liking for crowds, you will for the nth time (the nth time's a winner) promenade down the covered passages and avenues of the world's most varied, attractive bazaar. As you have found out in your haphazard wandering, a prospective customer venturing there will find, according to their fancies, mosques, barbershops, restaurants, chemists and a very wide range of objects from the ordinary to the unexpected and exquisite. The Great Bazaar is the reign of the improbable where everything is possible: I have even bumped into a Sephardic collector of coins bearing effigies of 'our king Juan Carlos' and an advertisement for a Goitisolo cognac displayed in an Armenian's shop window next to the crossed flags of the Basque flag, the *ikurriña*, and a colour photograph of the Basque football team!

Kapali Çarçi is a wood where Walter Benjamin would have enjoyed getting lost: the points of reference which, like pebbles scattered in my wake, I had established on previous stays, have finally been erased from my mind and I stroll through the spacious precinct not knowing my destination, or my itinerary. It has been a long process, but I have completed a whole different education.

The Baths

The collection of privileged spaces, framed in the area of texts with descriptive detail very similar to those on postcards, should include a few streets of Tophane or Kasimpaça with their romantic Ottoman façades, local squares with conciliar assemblies of cats, small parks in outlying districts where leather-breeched youths smeared in oil test out their strength, agility and skills on the eve of the Kirkpinar contests.

A last-minute visit to the archaeological or Islamic art museums might be timely, but with two *yagli güresceler* (greased or oiled wrestlers), both old friends of mine, we selfishly decide to fight off exhaustion from a day's urban trawling and subject ourselves to the ancestral purification ceremonies: the baths where we are heading have not the distinction of the Eskikaplıca of Bursa or of the great baths of Edirne, attributed to Sinan; nevertheless, they contain the elements and attributes of this national institution to which the citizens of the country have been addicted for years.

With a large towel from midriff to knees, after leaving clothes and belongings in one of the lockers in the hallway, the customer of the Sultan *hammam* cautiously enters a series of rooms with small cleansing fountains sunk in shadows. The baths properly speaking are covered by domes whose translucent skylights sift the light and surround the bathing rituals in an ineffable aura, in subtle shades of unreality. Stretched out on marble slabs, half a dozen individuals await the energetic intervention of the masseurs in a passive state of surrender. Sometimes, friends or mere acquaintances embrace and mutually pummel shoulders and backs to prepare muscles and tendons for the consummate labour of the artist. This physical familiarity – the strict opposite of alienation from the body accorded by jaded Puritanical morality – always surprises western travellers with their uptight, insecure notions of manliness. The play of hands is in no way rough or coarse: the natural innocence of the contact, even the shows of emotional tenderness, simply prove that no-one feels coerced by norms of would-be, inflexible masculinity. Submission to the arts of a skilled, well-proportioned masseur is one of the most refined of Turkish delights: from the soles of his feet to his skull and eyebrows, a foreigner will experience the different stations or degrees of a methodical, enhancing torture, becoming in the space of a daydream, a simple object of gentle and harsh, intense and refreshing sensations, till he reaches a state of unimaginable bliss – the happiness of someone trying out a new body as if it were a new suit. Dislocated, shattered, re-shaped, soaped from top to toe, bathed, wrung dry, comforted, head and waist wrapped in different sets of towels, wearing a turban made from fine material, led back to the restfulness of his bunk, plied with cups of hot tea or purest mineral water.

The *hammam's* employees have accepted the presence of a photographer in that temple dedicated to the glories of the body and in a friendly spirit allow themselves to be photographed after receiving their tip. 'Give Turkey some good publicity' one says as we leave. 'They make out we're the baddies, you know we're not.'

Cinema Eden

Postcards

Before saying a proper goodbye to the city at a Mawlana session of *sama* at the seat of the ancient Dervish brotherhood, the Professor of Spanish literature at the university presents me with a pretty little book *Eski Istanbul'dan, 'Kitap-Kart'*,* whose aims seem to coincide more than once with the text I am now concluding. The grand panorama of the metropolis, supposedly encompassing an almost infinite range of meaningful codes, has been rejected in favour of a whimsical, subjective, fragmentary collection of images of a Constantinople that no longer exists: murky, yellowing photographs of street-sellers of brooms, melons, sweet cakes, coal, toasted chickpeas; water-sellers, itinerant barbers, artisans, porters and even a group of *pompiers irréguliers* (a detail justifying a dream of their anomalous, undoubtedly exceptional aptitudes in contrast to those of the 'regulars'!)

Photographic or journalistic summaries for readers in a hurry cannot provide them with anything but the information they already possess. Those not satisfied by such redundancy will extend their apprenticeship in partial, successive forays. As Juri Lotman observed in the essay quoted earlier, the collisions provoked by superimposed layers of heterogeneous information predisposes the reader of the city conceived as a textual space, to a receptive, open attitude, in which the postcard assumes the role of a code of surprising richness and complexity. Istanbul, successively explored, recognised, assimilated, rectified throughout my fertile stays, is no longer for me but a collection or anthology of snapshots: its aggressive, prodigious, fascinating crowd renews and invents itself at each step like Heraclitus's river in a changeable, fluid continuity returning us to a glorious past, a voracious present and an indecipherable future.

---

* *Postcard Almanac of Old Istanbul*, introduced by Nezihe Araz, Istanbul, 1987

Strong Like a Turk

THE LEGEND OR, rather, legends on the subject leafily proliferate – pure verbal foliage, lithe lianas – in the area of poplars, riverbanks, streams and meadows sagely described by Góngora in the rustic contests of his first *Solitude:*

> The trees which had feigned the forest,
> Shape now a shadowy coliseum,
> Reveal the green,
> An Olympic platform
> For wrestlers naked and brave

To follow the most common accounts, some six hundred and forty-two years ago a bloody battle was fought in the outskirts of Edirne. Suleyman Pasha and forty of his men were at war in the interior of Thrace and camped on the shores of the Marilya. In interludes of truce, pressed by the sweet lethargies of summer, the soldiers put aside their weapons and donned a wrestler's leather breeches, and exercised their limbs in the arena of lush grass by the river. According to popular versions, two wrestlers felt such a burning desire to prolong the fight that, clasped in sinuous combat, vying in muscle and guile, they ardently pursued a chaste coupling in the moonlight, stout hearts syncopating, till exhausted they died: a divine dispensation, no winner, no loser. Their companions buried them under a fig tree, recited the traditional prayer to the dead in their honour and went off to war. Once the fighting was over, they returned to their friends' graves. When they reached the place where they lay they were astonished to find forty springs of the purest water pouring forth and called it Kirkpinar. They related the miracle to their commanders who surely ordered them to emulate such prowess, to lock handsome might in flights of flesh: 'Remove all your clothes and wrestle, to the glory of your comrades' souls, before the forty springs.' What happened next on the watery sand is not recounted by legend: the field was not feathers, the joust's rough virility enlivened no nuptials, no courting of shepherdesses, no battle of love.

Another lesser-known version relates the following: besieged by enemy troops, the Ottomans remained in the region of Edirne, cut off from supplies of food and weapons. Though in dire straights, their chiefs rashly agreed to hold a wrestling contest among the besieged to decide who was the strongest. Worn-out and hungry, forty warriors wrestled, clutched in hard, implacable embrace, till they surrendered their souls to God. The vast, plural fountain which spurted forth was surely their eternal reward.

After the Balkan wars, the place where the deed was regularly commemorated became part of Greece and the wrestling was curtailed; but, with the victory of Mustafa Kemal in the Turkish war of independence, Ataturk's new regime re-established the ancient tradition. Over the last sixty years, the *yagli* has been fought in the outskirts of Edirne, on the river island of Sarayici, popularly known as Kirkpinar. Early in June every year hundreds of wrestlers from the whole of Turkey gather to test out their vigour and skills, attracted by the idea of fame, honour and fortune, hoping to become national heroes and win the coveted *baçpehlivan's* belt.

*   *   *

The two hundred and twenty kilometres between Istanbul airport and Edirne spans the serene, fertile, often undulating Thracian landscape:

the road first passes the beaches of the Marmara sea, where thousands of bathers splash in quiet waters and, from the crossroads as the road forks, the taxi turns right to head diagonally from the coast towards the Bulgarian frontier. Field follows field of sunflowers, small pine woods afflicted by the malady of melancholy, frequent wire or metal fences warning of the nearby presence of military barracks or zones out-of-bounds to the public. There are numerous police or army checkpoints but, unlike on my last visit to the country, shortly after the installation of the 'new order', the vehicle won't be stopped and searched. Police and army seem absorbed in endless conversation and pay the traffic scant attention, abandoning it, like years ago, to the voluble inspiration of Turkish drivers. Mine seems to drive musically in rhythm to his favourite poet-singer: he accelerates, brakes suddenly, overtakes blind, ignores the continuous white line that theoretically should restrain his gleeful temerity. Softly humming his idol's words, he glides speedily between two huge lorries in a rush of wild, almost genial fantasy. But we reach Edirne in peace.

The provisional capital of the Ottomans during their long siege of Byzantium, ancient Adrianopolis was endowed by successive sultans with an exceptional array of monuments: the mosque of 'three galleries', with its twisted column of a minaret; the great baths attributed to Sinan the architect; the Bedestan and covered market; the caravanserai of Rustem Pasha where I was fortunate to stay on my previous visit; and particularly, the mosque of Selemiye, Sinan's masterpiece, a prodigious union of strength and slenderness, its airy, soaring minarets crowning the hill where it was built, always visible as landmarks from the meadows, streams, hillocks, riverbanks surrounding the city.

The modern town, victim to the constant trafficking of lorries to and from the Middle East and, at this time of year, of the colourful caravans of vehicles of Turkish workers driving from Germany or Holland, has nevertheless preserved a great part of its provincial charm:

small mosques, steep, zigzagging, cobbled side streets, overgrown gardens, miniature cafés, vine-shadowed patios, big, wooden houses, rustic barbershops, tiny urban cemeteries. Some corners remind me of the suburban Sarrià and Pedralbes of my childhood before, like so much of that reticent, romantic Barcelona, they were sacrificed in the name of progress to the fierce speculation of property developers. Similarly the centre offers numerous open spaces: gardens with kiosks, open-air cafés, broad pavements packed with people out for a stroll. The many groups of youths in sports gear or tracksuits indicate that wrestlers are arriving for the Kirkpinar contest. When night falls and the minarets of the Selemiye suddenly light up, the mosque stands out in the darkness with all the splendour of a four-winged candelabra.

*   *   *

The island of Sarayici where the championships are held is in fact a vast, welcoming grove of poplar trees surrounded by the often-parched tributaries of the modest, muddy Tunca. About a kilometre from the city, the traveller walks there downhill through well-preserved nineteenth-century districts and, upon reaching the bridge over the river's reeds and sludge, can turn to enjoy a splendid view of the minarets of the Selemiye in the bright light of morning or bloody streaks of twilight. On the other side, the huge isolated field, deserted in winter, offers a welcoming, shady haven to thousands of traders and bystanders who, in the days or weeks preceding the wrestling, camp there with their belongings, carts, cars, flocks of sheep and tents. At the other end of Sarayici, another viaduct leads to the villages on the outskirts; close by, but on the other shore, are the ruins of beautiful Ottoman baths that I didn't manage to photograph because of their proximity to army-manoeuvres territory. The guard who rushed to inform me was not persuaded by pleas of good faith or aesthetic motives: uniform, helmet, sub-machine gun and regulations got in the way. I bid farewell with a shrug of the shoulders and returned to the island's Babelian confusion.

The atmosphere on Kirkpinar is a mixture of a pilgrimage to a Moroccan marabout and an Andalusian religious procession: the fairground extends around the stadium and an onlooker wanders at ease, attracted by all kinds of show and spectacle, the patter of traders, rasp of loudspeakers, violent lashes of music. Tiny stalls selling tea and yogurt, rough awnings over beer and drinks pitches, restaurants roasting lamb on spits alternate with roundabouts, slides, huts selling wares or target-shooting, small tables with cartomancers, invariably blond and beautiful. Good-looking girls boldly accost passers-by with wooden hoops which if thrown expertly or luckily bring the eventual winner a wondrous packet of Marlboro. Tired families sleep peacefully next to their donkeys while in a nearby eatery several men dance hand in hand to the sound of a squeaky, squalid combo.

The stadium has been refurbished and extended, but its capacity can't cope with the mass of spectators who appear at its doors with tickets or determined to slip in gratis: its turf, high, lush, exuberant, like the grass on the meadows where the young men train, cushions and absorbs slippery, lubricious prey. The week before the trials, a band of bugles and drums, its members wearing sashes, turbans, knee-length breeches and striped shirts, their hammering beat sometimes evoking Spanish Good Friday processions, parades through the city morning and afternoon, subsidised by the dignitary who had purchased in an auction the honorary title of Aga. On the opening day, the leading wrestlers will walk in a cortège to offer the ritual wreath to Ataturk and pray the *fatiha* before the graves of two champions side-by-side in the small cemetery of Pehlivanlar. Hours later, the city seems to empty out and a stream of people converge from different paths on the rustic river arena for the jousts.

*   *   *

Cinema Eden

The names of the most distinguished *baçpehlivanlar* in the history of *yagli* are known throughout Turkey and memory of their deeds and victories nourishes the popular imagination. Photographs and likenesses of Koca Yusuf, vanquisher of European and American champions, of Hergeleci Ibrahim, Ali Ahmet or Mehmet and Kara Ali, winners over three consecutive years of the coveted gold belt – are still sold in markets and their names proclaimed in village festivities.

Curiously, despite the fervour surrounding the contests of Kirkpinar and its numerous heroes, *yagli* doesn't really enjoy the urban facilities that reflect its deep social roots. Training rooms are antiquated and scarce, wrestlers do not receive generous help from town halls or government and, outside the army, training centres often lack the most basic requirements. These circumstances explain why the temper and renown of young fighters is especially forged in village celebrations on the occasion of weddings or other family entertainments. There young men try out their strength and gradually learn the rules and techniques of engagement. Those who thus acquire an aura of prestige then risk outings with fighters from local villages and, later, from the capital of the province or *wilayat*.

A few years ago, Kirkpinar seemed to experience a period of irremediable decline and some conjured up the spectre of possible 'folklorisation'. Today, there is an evident climate of recovery: *yagli* wrestling – literally 'oily', 'greasy' or, if you prefer, 'annointed' or 'lubricious' – again confers a sense of pride and identity on the long-suffering mountain peasant. As the economic crisis in Europe closes the safety-valve of emigration, unemployed youths and workers dream like Spanish novice bullfighters about sudden fame and riches. Wrestling is almost the bullfighting of Turkey, with its attendant hopes and misery, desire for glory and real disappointments. Simultaneously, a box-office success, starring Tarik Akan – Yilmaz Güney's favourite actor – has in turn enhanced the prestige of *yagli* in urban centres: the sub-proletariat of Istanbul and Ankara saw itself reflected there. The combination of such factors explains why the confluence of spectators and wrestlers in Edirne has been exceptionally high this year. On the inaugural day of the competition, around a thousand candidates – boys, adolescents and young men – waited patiently on the grass, not yet dappled with oil, for the signal from the referees to fight the matches corresponding to their category.

*   *   *

The evening before the struggles I accompanied a select group of wrestlers to a field near the railway, at the other end of the city: Sabri Acar, champion of champions for 1985, and Bekir Sahin, Abdullah Ersoy, Zeyni Kaya, Nazmi Kendir, Fikret Demir and other figures from past and present competitions. Each of them carried a bottle of olive oil and soft, leather breeches, his *kispit*. The latter usually has a finely embossed pattern at the top both behind and in front, but no opening and it is tied round the calves with laces. The wrestler's first name or surname is printed on a level with the small of his back. Contrary to what one might think, the waist isn't fitted to the owner's size but is quite loose to enable the rival's arm and even forearm to be introduced as holds are established and it is consequently held by a cord. The front panel of the breech, also embossed, is opulent and assumes the bulging form of a scallop or luscious bunch of grapes: two decorative side buttons further emphasise the showy image of sturdy vigour. The *kispit* varies according to its owner's taste and means: the embossed work is sometimes intricate and reveals an artisan's patient, exquisite toil. In some cases it is home-made; but today they are predominantly from specialised tanneries and curers. Less fortunate wrestlers whose pockets don't allow such expense usually wear green, blue or greyish breeches made of very resistant canvas, known as *pirpit*: this is modelled entirely on the leather variety but never attains its emblematic impact and elegance.

Once the breeches are on – the operation to tie the leggings with small pieces of string is a rite which can take a good quarter of an hour – the wrestler opens his bottle of olive oil, carefully anoints torso and extremities and helps lubricate those of the comrade with whom he will test out his potential and reflexes. This mutual massage must be urgent and gentle, and leaves the opponent's body oily and slippery. As I will see in the Kirkpinar stadium, the greasing is completed in two phases: first, the contestants jostle around two boilers full of oil, rub their bodies, including their private parts, sportingly collaborate in the oiling of their neighbour or future rival; then, after being summoned by the referees and drawing lots, trainers appear with jars, pour the contents on the shoulders and backs of the competitors and lubricators and lubricated sink their hands down the part covered by the *kispit* to ensure optimal anointment.

The sight of the wrestler greasy from head to feet, in shiny, slippery breeches, is not only imposing and vigorous: it also assumes a beautiful luminosity. The Turk lovingly cultivates his strength – one of the etymologies of the word *türk* is precisely strong – but for the real lovers of *yagli* it is worth little if not subtly harmonised with balance and flexibility. Unlike more modern, popular forms of wrestling, *yagli* doesn't allow the use of the legs or holds below the belt. Its adepts cannot passively obstruct their opponent, touch his face, bite or pinch him. Although they introduce hands and forearms innocently beneath their rival's breeches to get a grip on his inside leg to lift him up, they must refrain from mistreating or even skimming his hidden jewels.

The Turkish manual I have to hand mentions the existence of thirty-three *yagli* positions (a figure distinctly inferior to the *Kamasutra's*!) but the fact is the national lubricious struggle depends above all on a rigorously personal struggle and on a set of simple, basic rules. An excess or lack of strength when executing a hold can upset a wrestler's plans and provoke his defeat. The *pehlivan* has to have an exact sense of balance in order to throw his adversary at the precise moment equilibrium is broken. In general, the ways to defeat the opponent can be reduced to five: lifting him up and holding him for a minimum of three paces; throwing him to the ground, leaving his navel exposed; putting him on his back and touching the soil; forcing him to concede from exhaustion; taking his breeches down and off (a sublime gesture the ungrateful gods denied me!). I did see one youth's *pirpit* disintegrate, but the referee generously gave him an interval to get a replacement and resume fighting: the youth rushed to the dressing-rooms and, like Caesar, returned and conquered.

A match in the Kirkpinar stadium mustn't last more than an hour. If there is no victory or defeat, the opponents are given a ten-minute extension. If then there is no outright winner, the referees have recourse to a points-system. In the unlikely case that the contenders are still level, there is the possibility of a second extension called *activity*. Whoever is the most active, will win. Despite the fact that specialists in *yagli* evoke famous examples of the latter, the entwining, almost amorous embrace of exhausted, half moribund wrestlers belongs rather to the legends of the remote heroes of Kirkpinar.

* * *

A packed stadium: judges, referees, wrestlers have recited their prayers, palms of hands outstretched, and the first row of contestants impatiently awaits the sign from the *cazgir*. Although there are nine classes of *annointed*, from the champions to boys barely five years old, assignment to each level isn't exclusively determined by age or weight. At the higher grades, the judges take into account knowledge, ability and experience: a youngster who enjoys these may easily defeat a colossus trusting to his sturdiness. The lower categories of boys and adolescents – there are several hundred of them – compete first and gradually leave the terrain free to middle and light-heavyweight groups. After the youthful encounters, the *cazgir* reads the name and place of origin of the wrestlers, recites a special prayer dedicated to the jousts and gives the sign for off.

The line of those selected by lots walks quickly along, gesturing austerely, abruptly, bringing to mind some primitive, atavistic ritual. The band of bugles and drums rhythmically accompanies their movements and sounds out obsessively throughout the combats. *Yagli* has no limbering-up exercises or gymnastics: the wrestlers stride, lift their arms up and down, half turn and salute their assigned opponent by lightly skimming their hand or knee. The length of this exchange of courtesies is aleatory and depends on the serenity and preparedness of the adversaries: whilst some are rapidly entangled in holds, others carry on salutations and gestures till they attain perfect liminal stasis.

The collective panorama at Kirkpinar is one of great brilliance and sumptuous beauty. Judges in caps, knee-breeches and white shirts, scrutinise the simultaneous progress of bouts, interrupt them in case of accident or injury and proclaim the winner, by raising his arm. Matches can last less than a minute or exceed an hour, if the referee so decides. Sometimes, for a very long interlude, the fierce fighters stay still, like branches, locked together: lubricated tendons and muscles glinting in the sun, their clasp seemingly eternal, awaiting the propitious moment to suddenly break the equilibrium. Bodies taut, arched, supple: simultaneity of tensions and embraces of slippery, serpentine texture. The ferocious, ardent moment calls for another reading of the *Solitudes*. As in the poet's rustic wedding, the sinuous, muscular rivals, *by reciprocal knots restrained, like hard elms by vines entwined*, vie in the air: at once nimble and robust. Their hearts' syncopated beat is transmitted to the spectators', vibrates in the air to the sound of drums and music. There is no more beautiful game or contest than Kirkpinar's at the much awaited conclusion to the bouts: the solitary final dispute of two champions – imbricated, clinging, panting – in the *murky embers of day*.

A brief glossary of Turkish wrestling

BAÇPEHLIVAN	Champion of champions. Pronounced *bachpelivan*.
CAZGIR	the announcer of the bouts in Kirkpinar. Pronounced *shazguer*.
GURIESÇI, GURESCILER	Wrestler, wrestlers. Pronounced *gurechshi, gurechshiler*.
KIRKPINAR	Place of the 'forty springs'. Pronounced *Kerkpenar*.
KISPIT	A wrestler's leather breeches. Pronounced *kespet*.
PEHLIVAN, PIEHLIVANLAR	Champion, champions.
PIRPIT	Breeches made from thick material, with the same features as a *kispit*.
YAGLI GURES	Literally an oily, greasy, or in the strict sense, lubricious fight.

The Whirling Dervishes

I was snow, your rays melted me;
The ground soaked me up; mist of the spirit
I rise up to the sun.

The Diwan of Shams Tabrizi, MAWLANA

DESPITE THE NUMEROUS TESTIMONIES collected by his relatives and disciples – by his son Sultan Walad, by Ahmet Aflaki and Sepashalar – and the scrutiny of modern writers, Mohamed Iqbal, Reynold Nicolson, John Arberry, Eva de Mitray-Meyerovitch, Mehmet Onder and Michel Random, the life of Jalal al-din Rumi, better known as Mawlana, is still graced by a legend fashioned from myth and reality. The handsome green dome that stands out sharply from Konya's slender minarets as startling as a mirage, shelters beneath its conical roof of Turkish tiles the remains of one of the world's greatest mystics, comparable in importance to Eckhart, to Hallax or Ibn Arabi, to John of the Cross or Teresa of Avila. The author of the famous lines:

Come, whoever you may be, come
Infidel, pagan or idolater, come!
Our door is not there to discourage
Though I perjure a hundred times, come!
Whether Farsi, Turkish or Greek,
Learn the language of those who have none!

was born sometime between 1190 and 1200 in the now defunct city of Balkh within the boundaries of Afghanistan. His father, Baha ud-din Walad was from a family of theologians and his religious and philosophical teachings earned him the honorary title of 'Wise among the Wise'. Nevertheless, some *ulamas*, who envied the power he wielded in the town, disagreed with his interpretations and accused him of undermining the sultan's power. Baha ud-din was hurt and wrote these lines to the monarch: 'Armies, thrones, treasurers, the mortal things of this earth, belong to kings. We are dervishes and need neither land nor sovereign power. We shall continue our journey pure in soul and shall leave the sultan his wealth and vassals'. He left Balkh in 1220, and shortly afterwards the Mongols destroyed the town and the entire kingdom of Khurasan. 'I leave God to go to God,' Baha ud-din Walad says on hearing the bad tidings. 'I come from nowhere and am going nowhere.' The small caravan of refugees fled before the armies of Genghis Khan, headed westwards across Persia and Mesopotamia and took temporary shelter in Syria. There Baha ud-din visited the famous mystic from Murcia, Ibn Arabi, who, so the story goes, saw Mawlana respectfully following his father down the street, and exclaimed: 'Miracle of god, an ocean walking after a lake!' When Baha ud-din and his followers had made their pilgrimage to Mecca, they settled in the city of Karaman, to the south of Anatolia, where young Mawlana married. In 1229, the Seljuk sultan of Konya, a great patron of the sciences and poetry, invited Baha and his family to come to his kingdom and generously places one of his schools, or *madrasas*, at his disposition.

Mongol devastation and blood-letting had produced panic and created in the countries under threat an atmosphere of profound spiritual anguish, fertile ground for the development of mystical ideas. Sufis, preachers, philosophers and wandering dervishes were welcomed by the religiously tolerant Seljuks. The town of Konya was a forum in which doctrine was disputed by both orthodox Sunnis and

Sufis of different schools, a place of fruitful freedom enjoyed by Shi'ites, Christians and Jews alike. For two years Baha ud-din worked unhindered as a theologian and preacher. Upon his death, Mawlana succeeded him as head of the *madrasa*. He made the journey again to Aleppo and Damascus and met poets and sages and then returned to Konya where he devoted himself to the study of literature, law and science, and began to write sermons and study Greek philosophy until he was known as a prestigious *ulama*, preacher and mufti. When his first wife died, the mother of his first born, Sultan Walad, and of Alah ud-din Chelebi, he married Kerra Hatun and had two more children. He was the spiritual leader of his community, famous for his sermons and *fatwas*, respected by monarchs and the people; the career of Mawlana – literally, Our Lord – seems set firmly on course when suddenly it is disrupted by an unexpected incident that radically alters his life.

Mawlana meets Shams Tabrizi and the meeting sweeps away his body of knowledge, his certain truths: like volcanic lava it carries all swirling before it. Through the many versions related by his disciples it is possible to see the event of 29 November 1244, 'the union of the two oceans', in a rich profusion of detail. According to one disciple, Shams the dervish bursts into the *madrasa*, throws Mawlana's books into a water container and responds to the owner's criticism by taking them out one by one, each perfectly dry, as if they have not suffered from their immersion: another relates how, while Mawlana is expounding his teaching to a group of novitiates, Shams enters the room and points at a pile of manuscripts and asks, 'What is this?' 'You know not,' Mawlana replies. Suddenly the volumes blaze into flames, and it is Mawlana who exclaims, 'What is this?' and the intruder who replies, 'You know not,' before he disappears. In a less fantastic account, Mawlana is riding his donkey to the bazaar, when a hirsute, ragged dervish, his eyes like fiery embers, seizes the donkey by the reins and clings on tightly with his naked arms. He blurts out two questions of a mystical nature. Mawlana replies and then falls delirious. Once he has come to, he takes Shams' hand, leads him to the *madrasa* and shuts them both in a cell for forty days.

Mawlana has discovered love. As Sultan Walad, his first son, later says, 'God allowed Shams to show himself uniquely to him . . . No one else had been worthy of such a vision. After waiting so long, Mawlana saw Sham's face; his secrets were diaphanously revealed. He saw he who cannot be seen, he heard what no one had ever heard from human lips . . . He fell in love and was annihilated.' To describe this experience of death and transfiguration Mawlana writes simply: 'I was raw, I was cooked, I was consumed.' The two mystics finally come out of their seclusion, which has been watched over by the young Sultan Walad, and go to the inauguration of a *madrasa*, where Mawlana is to speak. Curiosity and envy centre on Shams. While the wise and the worthy argue over which honorary place corresponds to them, the dervish crouches in the corner where the shoes are piled. Mawlana calmly pronounces: the wise men will sit on the couch, the mystics on the cushions and the man in love next to his friend. To the amazement of those present he goes over to the side of Shams Tabrizi, whom from that moment on he will call 'My Lord'. 'Love orders the universe,' Mawlana says, 'we are atoms, it is the ocean and we are mere drops of water.' Mediator and incarnation of occult understanding, the dervish sets Mawlana on fire. Mawlana establishes him in his library, welcomes him into the heart of his family, offers him the hand of an adoptive daughter, dedicates countless poems to him. Shams wrenches him from spiritual lethargy; he is the avatar for the unknowable deity. Mawlana has seen God in his wild, thorny form, which is how his cry of 'Oh Shams, oh my God!' should be interpreted. He scandalises the Islamic dogmatists by playing on Shams' name, meaning sun in Arabic – and writes: 'The sun of Shams' face, glory of Tabriz, shines on nothing mortal without making it eternal.' Mawlana abandons his sermons and *fatwas*, neglects his pupils, absorbs himself in mystical discussion, scorns all worldly respect and consideration. Mehmet Onder tells how the dervish, perhaps influenced by the concealed ethics of the transgressors or *malamatiya*, subjects Mawlana to a harsh test: to put an end to his pride he tells him to go and buy wine in the market. When Mawlana obeys and is publicly ridiculed, he throws the flask away and embraces him, moved by the manner of his greatness. Shams initiates his friend into the dance of the dervishes and the envious mutter, 'Who is this Shams who has snatched our master from us, and deprived us of his presence?' Is he a magician, an infidel, a heretic? Why has he led Mawlana astray, away from his studies, his piety and knowledge?' The day Shams' wife suddenly dies, the gossip becomes poisonous: only Shams can be responsible for the young girl's death. The dervish, a target of hatred and lies, leaves Konya on 15 February 1246, without warning Mawlana, and disappears.

When Mawlana discovers Shams has gone, he falls into a state of collapse. He takes refuge in poetry and begins to compose his *Mystic Odes* or the *Diwan of Shams Tabrizi*. He desires only that his departed lover reappear: if love is madness, he resolves to be a madman among the wise. He sends messengers out to look for him as he writes: 'I am afraid to visit the places where you walk, fearful of those who love you/ Day and night you live in my breath;/to see you I look at myself in the mirror'. 'Body laid waste', 'a thirsty traveller', 'a lonely recluse amid the ruins', he calls after, entreats his friend, when he hears he is in Syria, travels in vain to Damascus, and sends him servants and gifts. Back in Konya, inconsolable, he writes impassioned poems; entranced by mystic love, he dances hour after hour with the whirling dervishes. Sultan Walad, Mawlana's first born, makes a fresh attempt to find Shams. Guided by a beautiful dream he is successful. Walad prostrates himself at Sham's feet, gives him his horse, urges him to return. He tells him how the slanderers who include his younger brother, Alah ud-din Chelebi, have repented: the whole city anxiously awaits him. Shams relents, and the two mystics are reunited before the gates of Konya to popular acclaim and in the presence of the nobility. His hagiographers have recorded conflicting versions: some say Mawlana goes to greet his beloved and, as in their initiatory encounter, grasps the reins of Shams' mount; Aflaki and other disciples say Mawlana falls thunderstruck from his horse and returns to the *madrasa* in the dervish's embrace, where they dance the *sama* in celebration. Between 8 May and 5 December 1247, Shams stays by Malwana in perfect, mystical communion. In those months, the Sufi master writes some of the most beautiful compositions in his extensive, often challenging poetry dedicated to his friend's dazzling, solar presence:

> 'Object of my drunkenness,
> syllable on my tongue:
> without you, the planets are a prison;
> don't sleep yet, wait.'

The orthodox believers led, some say, by Mawlana's second son, are scandalised by the poetry's intimate tone, and plot Shams' death. On the night of December 5 they set an ambush for him, and now he vanishes for ever. Whether knifed to death by the conspirators or thrown down a well, his eclipse is a mystery that no one has unravelled to this day. Some think that Shams' corpse was exhumed and buried in Mawlana's mausoleum years after the latter's death. However, Mehmet Onder recently discovered some remains hidden beneath the burial place in the mosque dedicated to Shams in the centre of Konya. Whatever the truth may be, for centuries the dervish's sudden end had charged the magnetic power of his legend.

Mawlana's grief overwhelms him. Dressed in mourning, he can only find consolation in the *sama*, surrounded by dervishes and musicians. 'Separation', writes his son Sultan Walad, 'left him beside himself, love turned him head over heels. Once a sage and mufti, he became a poet; an ascetic, he was now drunk on love. Night and day he danced the *sama*, circling over the ground, spinning like the firmament. His mournful cries reached the Throne; both great and small heard his laments . . . He gave money to the musicians, and gave away all he possessed. For never a moment was he without dance or *sama* until no one was left to chant, all were silenced and worn out, unmoved by gold and gifts. All sick and weary, and without wine, in a haze of intoxication.' Although Mawlana, from whom the truth was piously hidden, does not see Shams again, he finds him thanks to the luminous path of poetry within himself. Once conjoined, he shares with him the brilliance of 'words of substance', as José Angel Valente writes of John of the Cross:

> Although far from him tangibly
> without body and soul we are an identical light.
> Look at him, if you wish; look at me, if you want
> seeker! I am he and he is I . . . Since I am he, what else
> could you be seeking? I am he, yet I speak of myself.
> I surely watch out for myself

After the experience of being *emptied* by the *Mystic Odes*, Mawlana signed his poetry with Shams' name: there is no difference between them; the lost dervish speaks through him. Converted into a symbol of divine love, his absence proves the reality of the world and has the power of reincarnation.

In 1249 another anagnorisis again wounds the poet with a shaft of light. One afternoon, after leaving his house, Mawlana crosses the goldsmiths' district and suddenly hears the beating of hammers shaping the metal. He catches the rhythm of the tools; the music transforms pain into ecstasy. He casts off his cloak, closes his eyes, turns toward the sweet harmony of the tapping, rests his head on his right shoulder and listens to the secret language of the metal-beater. The planets dancing around the sun gradually fuse with the thudding heart in his breast. Mawlana swings himself round, and as artisans and passers-by jostle to see him, one of the goldsmiths orders his apprentices to quicken their pace, to strike louder, louder till, losing all restraint he rushes over to dance with him. The gold merchant, though illiterate, imposes himself with the grace of possession. Henceforth it is he who comforts Mawlana in his cruel separation from Shams. Having surrendered body and soul to the way of *extinction*, Salah ud-din Zarkub, the gold-beater, renounces his worldly goods, shelters in the calm of the *madrasa* and becomes the poet's *new sun*, the one he calls Master among Masters and immortalises in his poems.

'Dance lightly, oh, Sufis, weave your ethereal circles!' Once more Mawlana lives intensely: Shams has reappeared in the countenance of the humble goldsmith. As before he binds him to his own family by marrying his loyal first son to Salah ud-din's daughter. The two men live in close union for ten years. If Shams' defects – his coarseness, fits of anger, liking for wine and other open defiance of religious law – had charged his opponents' spite to the point of causing his death, it is now the craftsman's rudimentary education that becomes the target of their hostility. Envy and gossip and failed assassination attempts do not however disturb the peace enjoyed by the two mystics, for whom only 'he who dies before dying really lives'. When Salah ud-din expires in 1258, Mawlana organises his funeral with all the hullabaloo of a wedding, carrying his corpse shoulder high as far as the tomb to the sound of flutes and kettledrums. Later, the master of Konya finds the light yet again in the person of Hasan ad-din Chelebi, a dervish belonging to his own brotherhood and fully versed in Sufi texts, to whom the poet dictates the six volumes of his *Masnavi*, an epic work encompassing all the different stages of his spiritual journey. Mawlana himself dies on 17 December 1273. As described by Aflaki in his colourful exposition of the master's deeds and words:

they had scarcely brought out his corpse on a stretcher than nobles and the people bared their heads; men, women and children, everyone came: the tumult of their voices sounded like the Resurrection. Everyone cried, and most of the men shouted and rent their clothes until they were almost naked. Members of different communities and nations had come together – Christians, Jews, Turks, Arabs, Greeks – each with their own holy book. In accordance with their customs, each repeated verses from the Psalms, the Pentateuch and the Gospels . . . readers of the Koran read beautiful *suras*, the muezzins melodiously chanted the prayer of the resurrection, twenty groups of musicians recited songs and poems composed by Mawlana.

And so the poet's desires were fulfilled, when he anticipated the attitude of his followers in the course of his last journey: *joyful, cheerful, drunken*, applauding his final meeting with the beloved. The *wedding night* of the great mystic has been celebrated ever since on the anniversary of his death, when a crowd of *mawlawis* and admirers gathers from throughout the world to worship in his tomb, in the famous mausoleum built within the precinct of the *madrasa*.

*   *   *

None of Mawlana's extensive, beguiling work, both in verse and prose, has been translated into Spanish; but any reader who is interested but ignorant of Farsi like myself, can consult the English translations by Reynold A. Nicholson and John Arberry, whose scrupulous faithfulness to the text does not deny the occasional successful poetic intuition. The mystic's works have been translated into Turkish, Arabic, German and other languages, and have been the subject of numerous studies, glossaries and commentaries, among which, as one might expect, the Hispanic contribution is conspicuously absent.

The nature of the lasting fascination of the *Mystic Odes*, the *Masnavi* and *Fihi-mafhi* is complex, many sided. As their interpreters have emphasised, the contemporary reader can only wonder at the visionary gifts that allowed him to divine, long before Copernicus and recent discoveries of physics and astronomy, the Earth as part of the solar system, the number of planets or the way each atom reproduces in miniature the whole of the cosmos. The dervishes' drunken whirl is the constant, dizzy round of the new stars:

> On, come, daylight, the atoms are dancing!
> The souls plunged into ecstasy are dancing!
> I'll whisper to you where the *sama* is going.
> All the atoms of the air and the desert
> You must understand, seem numbed.
> Happy or sad, each atom
> Falls in love with the truly ineffable sun.

The poet's daring images of the soul's path to perfection are close to those later formulated by other mystics like John of the Cross or Teresa of Avila; the open, ecumenical nature of his doctrine is a bridge that spans different cultures and epochs, unexpectedly drawing us nearer to him. The order of the dervishes was inspired by his life and writing, their definitive rules were written down by his son, and prescribe the rites of the dervishes exactly as they have reached us today, establishing for its members a framework of free thought, which without fanaticism, without breaking Islamic doctrine, seeks to find expression in the emptying of the inner self or ego through a combination of prayer, music and dance. The lapping of water, strains of the flute and the whispering hum of silence shaped the peace of the *madrasas* in the times of Mawlana: in the reign of the Seljuk sultans the insane were cured by the gentle harmonies of violins and flutes. The *mawlawis* do not accept the existence of insurmountable barriers between sects and religions, travel around in groups preaching poverty by example, scorning the symbols and attributes of worldly power. 'Be slaves, move over the ground like horses,' the master said. 'Don't try to raise yourself up on the shoulders of the people like a corpse being carried to the cemetery.' Although Mawlana's ambiguous language of love and extraordinary spiritual openness clashed with the dogmatism of some *ulamas*, his orthodoxy is not unworthy of the great mystic and jurist, Al Ghazali, whose work reconciles Sufism with strict faithfulness to religious law. 'In step to two rhythms,' Mawlana wrote, 'I place one foot firmly on the law while the other roams freely over the seventy-two nations [of the world].' Certain passages from the *Masnavi* seem to display a remarkably perceptive evolutionary conception of the universe: 'Man passed from the kingdom of the inorganic to the vegetable, without recalling his previous condition. When he reached the animal stage, he forgot he had been a flute . . . Later he reached the human condition, yet forgot his tender years. When he changes again he will transcend his present state.' But Mawlana attributes to *cosmic ascension* the nature of the spiritual itinerary or mental peregrinations of the Sufi masters: penetrate the ocean of divine love, 'in which your drop is transformed into sea.'

Although the doctrine of the mystic of Konya is no longer disputed by his compatriots, the words and actions of its initiator still arouse suspicion and criticism. Shams' often eccentric behaviour, described by his own disciples, seems to expel him to the antipodes of sanctity. He is bad-tempered and violent, he treats Mawlana roughly, he does not hide his fondness for gambling and is often rude to those who love him best. His attitude seems incomprehensible until it is related to the *malatiya* with its singular conception of the many paths to perfection. The spiritual lineage of the dervishes, just like the famous *kalandari*, whose Syrian-Christian origins have been established by Marijan Molé, rejects the good works and authority of pious, strict behaviour. The virtues of the *malamati* should be secret, and, in order better to hide them, he openly practises all that denies them.

By challenging conventional orthodoxy and public opinion, he draws nothing but scorn and censure upon himself, tames the pride in his soul, sacrifices appearances to the purity of his heart. Like the *malamati* Shams showed off his scepticism, he scorned prayers and rituals and when questioned by his followers, had the nerve to declare: 'Rosary, religion and convent are the law for ascetics; talismans, scepticism and taverns are the law for lovers.' As Random, Leconte and other scholars have pointed out, the dervish who inspired Mawlana probably belonged to one of the brotherhoods which for centuries had travelled the Islamic world practising dance, preaching poverty and abstinence, and sometimes professing an external amorality that made them popular with the people and the uneducated, deliberately outside the bounds of the religious establishment.

If nomadism, a notion of a journey that is both internal and external, is one of the keys of those who choose, like the light-footed, roaming Sufi, to fuse love and knowledge, the original meaning of the *sama* has not been entirely elucidated and is still the object of conflicting opinions. According to Molé it was practised by the primitive communities of Anatolia, Syria and Mesopotamia and must then have been spread through the Islamic world by alchemists and magicians, as a symbiosis of pagan love and mystical experience: its adepts would resort to the presence of youths whose lithe forms reflected divine beauty and brought on ecstasy. This custom, fiercely criticised by the enemies of Sufism – as was their use of opium, hashish and other drugs that induce trances and oneiric flights – was finally condemned by the devotees themselves as spurious and alien to their spiritual quest. The status of the *sama* was debated in a proliferation of religious literature over two centuries. Their adversaries accused the dervishes of hypocrisy, paganism and concupiscence; their prayers, some humorously commented, did not go further than the tips of their moustaches. But the work of Abu Hamid al Ghazali, whose brother was a famous Sufi poet and passionate defender of the *sama*, prescribed the criteria for the ceremony's performance and endorsed its legality. In his *Revival of the Religious Sciences* he examines in detail the rites of the dance and the relationship of the dances to the progress or stations of the soul, excluding anyone who is immature, the impure, the impressionable, anyone who might tear off their clothes and be unable to control hysterical outbursts. However, despite that, promiscuity, the presence of youths, drug taking and other rigorously proscribed activities would continue among groups of dervishes scornful of orthodoxy. When the traveller from Tangier, Ibn Battuta, visited Iraq he described in his *Rihla* a dance session in which the participants walked through flames and bit off the heads of snakes.

Nothing could be more alien than this fervour to the deep mystical meaning of the *sama* conceived by the master of Konya. The circular dance, as shown by Shams, was the true symbolic axis of his doctrine. The divine intoxication to which it aspires mirrors the order of the universe, the gyrations of the world and of the planets. Life, time, stars rotate in a perpetual dance: to commune with them you join in the *sama*.

> Why cling to the earth like a green plant?
> Aren't your movements the key to grace?'

Only he who chooses the way of union will be able to discern the secrets of nature. To become light, the lover must be reduced to shadow; before the illumination sought by the spirit, darkness is infidelity:

> Our intoxication does not need wine,
> Nor our assembly lutes or harps.
> Without orchestra or flute, wine-pourer or ephebe,
> We shall be drunk and elated, inebriated friends!

The *sama* was described by Sultan Walad and later discussed and elucidated by his descendants. The *Treatise on the Mawlawi ceremony*, by Mehmet Chelebi, the major reference for all scholars, includes a beautiful invocation of its mystical substance:

> A moth enraptured by his light
> Night and day, insanely, I burn away
> A wolfhound at his door,
> I am loved by the world.

Over time, the congregation of the *mawlawis* gained in power and riches what it lost in authentic simplicity. From the eighteenth century, the Chelebis enthroned the Ottoman monarchs, and were privileged to present the sultan with his sword. After spreading throughout the vast empire, they suffered from its degeneration, and, three years after the abolition of the caliphate, the father of the new Turkey abolished the order of the *Mawlawis* and all its brotherhoods and monasteries.

* * *

Arrival in Konya after the journey across the scorched, abandoned *meseta* is a real pleasure. One leaves behind the images and impressions of the capital created by Ataturk: severe, imposing buildings, Prussian rigidity, pedestrians and traffic veiled in mist, restrained bustle, a feeble sun, cold, sharp edges. Snapshots from two days of walking the streets: silhouettes in threadbare coats appearing and disappearing in the haze, unshaven faces, piratical expressions, brusque gestures, extinguished cigarettes hanging from lips, masticating jaws, struggle for survival, human steamroller, savage devouring of sandwiches, rough virile beauty, hard features, shadowy eyebrows, bushy profusion of moustaches.

Like Bursa or Edirne, Mawlana's adoptive town offers the curious traveller a variety of monuments as splendid as those of Istanbul. On my second visit to the city I easily found my way about and returned unhurried to the places that seduced me years ago: the forest of columns in the sober Arab mosque of Ala ud-din, now being fully restored; the great *madrasa* of Karatay, its dome open to the night's gleaming constellations through a central cupola, to the delight of any novitiates, keen astronomers and astrologers; the *madrasa* of the Slender Minaret, also erected by Seljuks, whose blue enamelled tower was struck by lightning, and especially the mosque and convent of the order of the whirling dervishes which has now been turned into a museum, the resting-place for the remains of the founder and his family. The organisers of the commemoration of Malwana encouraged me to explore places linked to the poet's life, to go on an excursion to Karaman, where Mawlana lived during adolescence, and to visit one of the mosques where there was once a monastery belonging to his order, its tiny cells open to the public.

The present status of the dervishes in Turkey is ambiguous. The *larikas* (brotherhoods) and *tekkes* (convents) were abolished sixty years ago: officially they do not exist. Conscious of the *mawlawi* legacy, the leaders of the new lay state are nevertheless striving to preserve its cultural dimension: the dervishes of Istanbul and Konya comprise two music and dance groups whose rituals attract devotees of the *sama* from numerous countries, and for this reason they are often sent abroad as a showcase of the artistic riches of Turkey. So the *mawlawi* ceremony survives in this ever fascinating but somewhat mediated form, and forces anyone who knows the life and work of Mawlana to ask himself and others a number of questions: doesn't the reduction of ascetic experience to a purely aesthetic act undermine to some extent the premises on which the *sama* is based, the mystic glow of its fire, the vertiginous, intimate fusion of knowledge and love? Doesn't the initiatory value of the dance perhaps fade when it is turned into a spectacle, into a cultural export, a tourist asset? Do those who now practise the *sama* preserve Sufi ideals, or do they merely perform gestures and rites like professional actors?

From my conversations with the dervishes in Konya and my observation of the Mawlawi ceremony held in the old convent at Galata I have not been able to reach any conclusions, confronted as I was by two contradictory experiences and by the use of a double language ridden with reservations and assumptions. Accepted as a legacy from the past and exploited as a tourist image, some dervishes reluctantly agree to being ascribed to folklore, preferring that to outright censorship. The annual anniversaries of the *wedding night* of the great mystic, and cultural exchanges with Europe and the United States gives them a chance to meet and unleash their Sufi inclinations without infringing the law. The popular fervour aroused by Mawlana – the devotees who on cold December days go and pray in his mausoleum, stretch out their hands in accordance with the norms of Islam, then hold them delicately to their faces as if to spread around the grace and virtue they have received – shows without a shadow of doubt that his spiritual influence has persisted.

The *mawlawis* I talked to in the dressing-rooms of Konya sports stadium, where they were getting ready for their dance, declared unequivocally that, although they did not live in a separate community or practise celibacy, they felt that they were dervishes within themselves and tried to adapt their morality and behaviour to Mawlana's precepts and teachings. As I was to discover, not all the members of the association which sponsors their performances share this same philosophy or their generous spirit: the attempts by my companion, the photographer Coskun Aral, to organise the *sama* in a more suitable setting were forestalled by the association's impossible economic demands. However, whether commercialised or not, the *mawlawi* ceremony survives: any fortunate spectator experiences in turn the happiness, entrancement and surrender that, according to the Sufi poets and masters, overpower even those who are mere eyewitnesses.

The ritual of stripping off civilian suits and slipping on the habit – the white blouse, waistcoat and bell-shaped skirt, the coloured sash the dervishes use to bind themselves together, the cotton robe they wrap majestically round themselves, and finally the ochre fur cylinder higher than a Cossack hat or the hood of a Holy Week penitent – follows a liturgy which at times evokes that of bullfighters: adults and novitiates kiss their caps before putting them on: they become self-engrossed, alien to all around, or talk quietly with friends and followers who have come to greet them. Among the visitors, they tell me, is Ahmet Ohzan, a famous actor and singer who has just given up his career in order to become a Sufi.

The Konya *tarika*, still directed by Chelebis descended from Mawlana, is made up of singers and musicians, the old *chij*, or master from Istanbul, and twenty-six dervishes aged between thirteen and fifty-five: the adult cloak is black, but two youths wear a blue one and the youngest is in green. Some of the faces of the dervishes, while they are waiting on their benches, unaware I am looking at them, have a rough, disturbing beauty. Workers, traders or artisans have been subtly transformed into something different. The austere habit of the brotherhood endows them with an emblematic glow: it seems suddenly to give them a halo, an irresistible impression of pride, rigour and calm.

By the time I wrench myself from this spectacle and slip on to the ugly basketball court where the *sama* is going to be performed, singers and musicians have already gathered in the area opposite their master's sheepskin, which, though tiny, solitary and pathetic, points, of necessity, to the *qibla*, in the absence of the octagonal room, with its pulpit or *mimbar*, and the recess or *mihrab* traditionally decorated with stalactites.

*   *   *

As I was to witness the following day in Istanbul, the Konya sama is enacted with slight variations in accordance with a centuries-old rite.

The dervishes enter the room opposite the spot where the master will stand, move forward very slowly in single file and line up to the right of the entrance next to the balustrade or barrier separating them from the audience. The white of their tunics symbolises the shroud; the black cape they wrap around themselves, the tomb; the brown cylindrical hat, the stela or funeral column that crowns gravestones in Ottoman cemeteries. The *chij* – his hat tied with a turban – walks behind them and heads towards the skin or mat opposite the musicians. Masters and dervishes solemnly greet each other with a nod of the head, then settle down on the floor, absorbed in meditation. The session begins with the chanting of prayers: *suratas* from the Koran, poems by Mawlana, a special oration for the prophet. Suddenly, a singer, in the purest of voices, intones the praises to Muhammad, written by Wallal ad-din Rumi himself, a stately chant, austere yet dazzling. The lead flautist improvises a melody on his ney, and the other musicians join in the prelude, anticipating the short signal to begin, a tap from the old man. Immediately, the dervishes respond loudly, lower their heads to the ground, rise up in unison and, led by the guide or *samaz*, bow in turn to the master before circling once, twice, thrice, round the court in an anticlockwise direction. At the end of these circumvolutions, the *chij* stands up, steps a few paces forward to the left (point one) of the sheep skin, gives a hint of a bow and, without losing sight of the skin, finally stands to its right (point two). The guide then walks to point one once occupied by the master, exchanges a greeting, and both embark, in slow cadences, on the previous whirling movement around the court. In turn, the dervishes imitate their expressions and gestures: move from point one to two, bow to each other, and form a silent chain behind them until the circle is closed. The wheel gyrates three more times: after the last turn, the dervishes return to their places, and the old man to his skin or mat. To the Sufis, these rotations symbolise the stations on the path that leads the immature soul to the bliss of knowledge and annihilation.

Flautist, musician and singers strike up again, and with the exception of the *samaz* the dervishes suddenly throw off their capes, keeping only their white habits and cylindrical hats. The guide goes to point one his right hand resting on his left shoulder, and vice versa. He respectfully kisses the master's hand and, after receiving his silent acknowledgement, steps to his right, inside the circumference from which he must direct the bi-orbicular movement of the whirling dance. One after another, their hands crossed over their shoulders, the dervishes greet the old man, seem to be set free from their invisible chains, stretch out their arms right palm upward, left palm downward, lean their heads to the right and begin to dance.

Although already seen in dozens of drawings, engravings and photos, the *sama* of the Konya dervishes arouses a sense of creative fulfilment, one to be compared only to that ephemeral power of the act of writing when it unexpectedly accedes to a state of grace: a vertiginous round, a drunken dance, a feathery lightness. The dervishes spin like tops, their tunics forming Saturn's rings, the white whirling folds turning into levitation. Following the guide's directions, they join one or another of the orbits of the planets, go from equinox to solstice, winter to summer: skies, stars, earthly elements evolve as weightless as an atom, their ebb and flow that of souls subject to the universal pull of the sun. The flute or trumpet blast of resurrection has dragged them from their tombs: the mystic *journey* of the dervishes goes, according to the Sufis, from the east of being to the west of non-being, from the west of non-being to the east of God. Vortex, immersion, drain, the dance annihilates illusory existence, allegorises the stages of ascent to dispossession.

It is not my intention to set out the wealth of interpretations and complex symbolism of the *sama* but to point to the artistic mastery and the emotion it communicates to the spectator. The whirling movement of the dervishes brooks no comparison with other dances: nothing could be further from the stylised drama of Spanish flamenco or the genteel perfection of ballet. The dervish surrenders to inebriation with ineffable lightness, his hands languish like withered petals, eyes turn blind, floating head, hands as if drowned in the ethereal air. Snowflake, planet or atom, he delicately gyrates around himself, in silent orbit around the absent sun.

Obeying the music's rhythm the dance is broken off three times, when the master greets the dervishes and invites them to continue to rotate. When, to the notes of a gentle flute, he in turn joins the circle, the Sufi's inner communion is consummated: the ceremony is nearing its end. Whirling dervishes return to their seats and don once more the black capes they had cast off. After a fresh reading of the Koran, the prayer in honour of the prophet and chanting of the Fatiha, the master bows his head still more, and, followed by heretic dervishes, majestically abandons the hall.

*   *   *

The famous *tekke* or Mevlevihanese in the present Museum of Classical Literature in Istanbul, situated at the top end of the unruly alley that cuts down through the district of Galata, zigzagging past its tower, the old Sephardic synagogue and the bustle and colour of the street with flat-roofed houses, finally spilling out into the chaotic hubbub of the Karaköy bridge and the quaysides of the Bosphorus, comprises an octagonal room with a pulpit and *mihrab*, columns with Corinthian and Ionic capitals, carved wooden banisters and a raised platform with shuttered windows, one of the balconies of which, opposite the *qibla*, is traditionally occupied by the musicians during the *sama*.

The session I attend, together with a select, cultured bourgeois audience, a vestige of Francophile Constantinople, is in two parts: a concert of Sufi music and a performance by the dervishes. Instrumentalists and musicians first occupy the centre of the room: the extraordinary virtuosity of the flautists, the players of lutes, violin or kettle drums allows one to appreciate in a proper setting the spare beauty of the melody and predisposes one to hear Mawlana's poetry. In turn, sometimes in chorus, the singers modulate their bell-line voices, and happiness, or rather ecstasy, overcomes the listener. The Sufi concert reaches an intense degree of austere, naked purity. Their liturgy pursues ascesis and sublimation, distils and equips the spirit for mental immersion in the dance.

But the Istanbul dervishes do not make the same impression as the Konya ones: their haste or ineptitude as they reach towards that ethereal state of abandonment and dispossession of the self required by the *sama* proves in my eyes their immaturity and lack of preparation. Apart from their guide, whose lead to the whirling dervishes, impelling them from one orbit to another, is proud, stirring and delicate, the group's members are like actors who do not live the ceremony from within: for some mysterious reason they lack grace and magnetism.

Is it the fault of the dervishes or of my exhaustion after a long, tiring journey? After leaving the *tekke*, I return to my hotel and re-read Mawlana. 'He who sees and he who is seen,' he tells me, 'become one within yourself.' A fortnight later as I write these lines, I am still unsure of my judgement or of the accuracy of my vision.

EGYPT

The City of the Dead

'The city rules over vast territories and fertile lands, is brimming
with inhabitants and can be proud of its beauty and splendour. A
meeting point for travellers and itinerants, a place for weak and
strong, where you can take your pick of men who are foolish and
wise, serious or light-hearted, complaisant or stupid, humble or
noble, blue-blooded or plebeian, unknown or famous. Its citizens
pound back and forth like the waves of the sea, hardly fit into its
seemingly narrow confines, though they be broad and
capacious. It enjoys eternal youth and is ever watched
over by the star of good fortune.'

IBN BATTUTA, *Description of Cairo*

WITH A LOOK LIKE THAT of a scrawny, furless, grimy, whimpering
cat, abandoned in the gutter amid the rapid procession of legs and
the deafening noise of traffic – whose squalid corpse we shall fatally
stumble across hours or days later, the victim of some vehicle's brutal
power or of a more insidious form of urban aggression – from his
precarious perch on the inhospitable road island of pavement slabs
and stones, alone in the flux of implacable chaos, the old man's
hazy, almost veiled gaze runs over the metal walkways packed with
people, the human tide rushing to attack the buses, the pedestrian
army confronting the din of screeching engines, the incessant bustle of
an entire people that, with efficient economy of movement, takes
advantage of the scarce space conceded to bodies to rush frantically
after the usual places of rest or activity, calculating perhaps like the
abandoned animal, through bleary eyes and shadows, the reprieve it

greedily enjoys, the breathing space destiny has granted to its precarious existence in an agglomeration where pavements have disappeared, the ground is crumbling on all sides, drivers respect neither lights nor policeman's whistle, a megalopolis cruel to the infirm and the aged; a city without pity, master, his eyes tell me, eyes now blurred as they meet with the insistence of mine; merciless, that's right, *bidun rahma.*

Why did I communicate for a few moments in silence with that old man, that particular old man before plunging in turn into the river of cars and selfishly abandoning him to his uncomfortable refuge? It all began a few hours before: the air-plane has flown over the island of Crete and is heading south, towards the Egyptian coast. From my window in the no-smoking area I have spotted God the Father indolently stretching out on the cottony eiderdown of a cloud: he seems in a good mood, is having fun with his cherubim and graciously points the pilot in the right direction like some mischievous, bantering car-park attendant who has just pocketed his tip, straight on, keep straight on. By nightfall I am in Midan al Tahrir: the taxi drove across the huge residential areas of Heliopolis and Masar al Guedid, headed up the avenue separating the university mosque of Al Azhar and the famous Khan al Khalili and, from the loathsome motorway raised up on two levels in a futile attempt to ease the traffic flow, I fleetingly contemplate, as in a slide-show, the unmeasurable sprawl of the catastrophe below hidden by the advertising hoardings for Coca-Cola, Seven Up and Marlboro: decrepit housing, buildings walking a tight rope, balconies on the point of collapse, domes held up by a miracle, dust, dirt, poverty, clothes spread out to dry, children hanging out of windows, faded publicity posters, terraces covered in shacks, chicken-runs, rubbish, pigeon lofts, aerials, herds of goats.

Violent images of a city's distorted face with its wrinkles, cracks, scars, glazed eyes, bruises, sores, black eyes, sticking-plasters, patches, broken teeth, dislocated jaws, whilst my taxi drives towards the

Ezbekiya gardens, above Midan al Ataba, between buildings whose splendour has faded and worn. The turrets and balustrades of a rococo edifice seem to have softened and melted like icing! On the dome of the old Tiring department stores four titans effortlessly hold aloft a glass terrestrial globe which has shed panes of glass like withered petals!

The airborne motorway has finally turned into the hurly-burly where bumper to bumper, hundreds of vehicles give vent to their owners' impatience with piercing blasts on the hooter. Pedestrians apparently accept the situation, too exhausted and weak to rebel against the perennial acoustic assault, the violence of traffic, in a state of shock. If Sir Richard Burton observed a century and a half ago that the lively gestures and exchanges of the people of Cairo might lead a foreigner to the mistaken belief that they were always within an ace of coming to blows, nowadays gesticulating is a necessity imposed by the unbridled ferocity of the traffic. The traveller who assails a taxi-driver, clings to the window, demands the presence of a policeman, challenges the edgy bustle of the crowd, insists on an on-the-spot fine for the man whom, he maintains, has insulted him, mimes a silent scene, shut out by the din and uproar. We must get on!

The journey to the hotel takes on dreamlike hues, swathed in a cloud of fantasy. The multitude hanging on the doors of trams and buses reflects the frenetic growth of a city that in ten years has gone from seven to fourteen million souls. Meanwhile the excavations for the underground railway have opened up the monster's entrails, generating fractured drains and mephitic floods, intensifying the general, irremediable confusion. In the centre drivers attack the cross-roads as if in fairground dodgem cars. A tanned, weasel-faced policeman waves his puppet arms to no avail, tries to halt a powerful Mercedes that drives right round him transforming his frustrated attempt at interception into a tardy, reluctant gesture of authorisation. My taxi has stopped next to him and I observe at leisure his threadbare uniform and bulging crotch, his would-be air of authority, the cynical expression of an impotent ruler over chaos. The human bunches hanging from the carriages of the Helwan train have crashed into those coming from the opposite direction: six dead! Not a single building in Cairo has fallen down this week though fifty per cent of them are in a state of ruin. But the city is still not Calcutta, the rats have not yet invaded the houses, beggars and cripples do not yet display their horrible stumps in hotel entrances, nor are they whipped out of sight by uniformed porters, the people is not yet dying on the pavements, walking skeletons do not yet proffer their lifeless hands or force the foreigner afraid of treading on them to jump to one side. My arrival at the hotel where I am to stay was merely an interlude in this initial vision of Al Qahira – literally, the Victorious – into whose omnivorous, emetic belly, I shall stride minutes later. The city that absorbs me is the ubiquitous, unleashed monster described by Edward Jarret in his excellent novel. For a few hours my gaze will be that of the old man sheltering on the traffic island: the disillusioned lucidity of someone who knows his sentence and is calculating the time left before he is blotted out.

*   *   *

In those ineffable Egyptian television serials, destined to stifle and dull the intelligence and sensitivity of Arab peoples, the directors carefully fashion the ideal ambience in which the plot will unravel: enormous apartments, modern offices and shops, peaceful gardens and walks the silence of which will be broken at most by whispering couples or soothing bird trills. Ordinary people have been unceremoniously expelled from those empty, hermetic spaces. Nothing indicates the proliferating human warren of the city: just shots of a deceptively clean river, private parks, avenues as bourgeois and exquisite as the characters' cars and houses. A utopia, a drug fantasy, a need to compensate for the cramped, promiscuous life of millions of people condemned to overcrowding in their lives as well as in the street? Do these women, men, children, old people who buy, sell, beg, work, eat and sleep on packed pavements nourish their dreams of a better life on the vision of those spacious rooms with showy furniture covered in grotesque fabrics whereon the dolls of the day strive to prove to them that 'The rich also cry' with grimaces and mimicry that would make the worst provincial actor in Spain blush with shame. I decided to walk in the opposite direction along the Al Azhar avenue where I drove by taxi the previous evening, and followed the capricious inspiration of my footsteps along the side-streets of Al Ghuriya, on the way to Khan al Khalili. The television counterpoint to the urban mass through which I cut a path, which I dodge as best I can, and which I inevitably knock and bump into, is suddenly sharply recalled, glaringly confirmed: a carpenter and two apprentices are putting the last touches to a paradigm of television furniture, one of those gilded armchairs, covered in plush or red velvet, with curved backs and huge seats, purpose-built, one could say, to greet stout bourgeois behinds, jubilant pontifical buttocks. As I turn my smitten gaze away from the purple throne I exultantly discover dozens of others lining up. The whole street is manufacturing tawdry furniture whose natural destination will be the lounges, repeatedly displayed on television, in the villas and apartments of the new class enriched by the *infitah*! On subsequent days, as I roam around the poor districts of Al Muski and Bab al Jal, on every corner I will come across new specimens of this armchair, whose unmistakable style I shall dub Louis XXVI to distinguish it from the other Louis: the beneficiaries of Sadat's unbridled opening-up of the economy would easily confuse the dynasties of Pharaohs with the list of our Gothic kings!

Hardly have I got over my discovery than I must step to one side to give way to a funeral cortège: the first of those I will have an opportunity to witness later during my stay in the City of the Dead. Friends and relatives of the deceased take turns to transport the coffin on their shoulders with a swaying, almost dance-like rhythm; at the rear women rigorously dressed in mourning also accompany the bier but without gesticulating or wailing. Minutes later, by the door to a mosque, I will come across another funeral retinue in which women mourners seem to rival and spur each other on to greater moaning and sobbing. I am now on the outskirts of Al Azhar and, through the pedestrian subway, I reach Khan al Khalili and the vast, well-tended esplanade next to the Hussein mosque. On the terrace of one of the cafés, from my seat amongst the *narghile* drinkers – in Egypt and Turkey, the same verb (*charab, igmek*) means both drinking and smoking – I can comfortably observe the spectacle of the multitude going in and out of the sanctuary, the door of which has been sheathed in a black canopy on the occasion of the celebration of *mouloud*.

The square has been closed to traffic and the parking of vehicles, but after a brief discussion and a tip to the wardens, some taxi drivers get the privilege of driving up and stopping next to the mosque. I notice straightaway that the passengers are newlyweds accompanied by a small number of friends and relatives. An old Cairo custom requires a ritual photo of the betrothed in the entrance to the Hussein mosque. The girls, daubed with rouge, *khol* and lipstick, look like models in Pronuptia sales items: skirts with long or half-length flounces, gauze headdresses, spotlessly white stockings and shoes. The men sport modest off-the-peg suits and clumsily fiddle with their bow ties. Policemen, soldiers, passers-by tirelessly watch fresh taxis arrive, the to-ing and fro-ing of the boys who open the car door for the fiancée with her sprig of flowers, the groups of hired singers, the swarm of photographers ready to immortalise that moment of joy. The small groups rapidly follow each other and the pretty, young bride can point a brief withering look of contempt at an elder, lean well-endowed companion. The mosque porter – a young man in a white tunic, with black turban and beard – waits leaning on his broom-handle, next to the marble lobby where the betrothed must take their shoes off before visiting the temple. His mission is to clean the dust zealously from in front of the bride's feet in exchange for a tip. This labour, the exclusive rights to which he defends with might and main, obliges him to push the dirt from one corner of the doorway to another throughout the day as new candidates for a photo turn up, but – and this is vital – without ever removing it completely, as its existence is indispensable to the completion of his task. Broom in hand, he hurriedly sweeps the corner where the bride steps, energetically repelling the dust to the opposite side, and reverses the operation when the next group arrives. Thanks to a quantity of mobile if constant dust, the wily fellow never ceases to tuck away 25 or 50 piastre notes, perhaps even a pound, into the depths of his coat pocket with an expression of humble, entranced bliss. His presence in the midst of fiancées, relatives, morons and photographers, clasping his emblematic broom like some fairytale witch, turns him into a character in a comedy by the Quintero brothers or in the zarzuela, *The Barber of Lavapiés*.

In any case, the spectacle of plebeian weddings in the Hussein mosque makes a pleasant contrast to the pompous *nouveau riche* ceremonies in the Hilton or Sheraton. As I had occasion to testify on a previous visit to Cairo, caricature there soars to unexpected heights, whilst never attaining the redeemable vulgarity of *kitsch:* the wedding cohorts process slowly to the light of fake beacons, applauded by a hired gang of waiters and lackeys; a film director shoots the different episodes of the festive event – the obligatory close-up of the bride's jewels – that will be shown later on video to visitors to the newly weds' sitting-room, furnished, of course, with Louis XXVI *fauteuils*. The pious, bearded sweeper would indeed introduce a bright splash of colour. But the closed world of the well-to-do – refractory and hostile to contact with ordinary people – does not readily allow this kind of intrusion.

As I walk back to my hotel, along the crammed streets of Al Muski,

Cinema Eden

I mull over the reasons for my already long-standing love of Cairo: unlike European or North American cities, where one grows old at life's edge, reduced to a robotic state with semi-atrophied feelings, a short stroll through the insect-like bustle in the centre puts the traveller into immediate contact with the roots of life. Within a few hours I have seen dozens of weddings and two funeral cortèges! My sense of smell, blunted in cities subjected to anaesthetising asepticism, gradually comes back to life, aroused by the violence of the smells! No matter if the scent of flowers, spices or cedar wood mingles with that of excrement or rubbish. I am alive, I am walking around a *medina* where everything happens in the light of day and something is happening all the time. Is the degradation of the urban space – public works' trenches, aerial motorways, clapped-out yet over-laden buses – just a mirage? As one of its recent visitors* perceptively notes, doesn't this apparent dislocation, self-destruction and decay perhaps constitute 'a perpetual, cunning exercise in the redistribution' of its materials? Sinking down to get better foundations, falling apart to rise up, sicking up its detritus in order to devour even more. Doesn't Cairo, excessive and cruel, ragged and magnificent, feed, century after century, on the marrow of its children in a perennial, mocking exercise in self-consumption? I re-read Ibn Battuta and his political diagnosis of the city: 'The military tyrannise; the poor people suffer; but the powerful are not disturbed and the machine works as best it can'. Is there a better way to sum up the history of the last fifty years? I have yet to climb the spiral staircase up Ibn Tulun's minaret to enjoy the perfection of a mosque which can only be compared in the elegant purity of its lines to the Koutoubia in Marrakesh, yet the city has already reconquered me. Destroyed, ruined, burnt, tentacled Phoenix, *mantis religiosa*, Cairo seems to have discovered the secret of a continually renewed cycle which mingles life and death until they are fused.

* Sami Nair, *Le Caire, la Victorieuse*, Paris, 1986.

If the cemetery is the city, as the Spanish Romantic Larra said, we will have to go right to the heart of the macabre to explore its sources of life.

*   *   *

The same imprecision concerning the name of Egypt – known by its offspring both as Berr Masar and Bilad Masar – and its capital – called indistinctively Al Qahira or more simply, Masar – also surrounds the siting of the legendary City of the Dead. While Burton situates it in the Bab Naser cemetery, my tourist guide locates it in Qait Bey and keenly advises against visiting for reasons of 'decency'. Cairo has in fact had for centuries four remarkable Muslim cemeteries as well as the Coptic cemeteries and a Jewish one: Bab Masar, Qait Bey, Bab al Wasir and Al Khalifa, or belonging to the *imam* Chaafai. The latter, equally dubbed the southern cemetery of Bab al Qarafa, has today more in common than the others with the features of a residential necropolis. Although I have leisurely trawled the mausolea, tombs and funeral pavilions of Bab Masar and Bab al Wasir, the number of Cairenes established there is relatively small and, in some areas of the latter, almost insignificant.

Qait Bey, famous for the splendid mosque to which it owes its name, is a special case. The population of the urban centres established in the macabres, and the one which traditionally looked after the pantheons, increased dramatically twenty years ago with the massive influx of refugees from the left bank of the Suez Canal, suffering at the time from merciless Israeli bombing raids. This take-over, ratified by the impotence of the authorities, turned the cemetery into a city which presently boasts more than half a million inhabitants: with its mosques, schools, hospital, administrative buildings, markets, it constitutes an autonomous agglomeration whose precarious living conditions are expressed in a melancholy succession of images of overcrowding and poverty. In the square adjacent to the eponymous mosque – in a somewhat unreal setting of small stalls selling lupins and a ghostly, home-made roundabout – a handful of writers and artists whom I am unsure whether to describe as populist or *maudits* meets up in the afternoons in a café to inhale the smoke of narghile (*chicha*), fortified, to be true, with small cubes of hashish.

Qait Bey, or north eastern cemetery, in spite of the varied interesting aspects of its appeal to the curiosity of casual visitors – hundreds of mausolea, sometimes built with stones of the Pharaohs, raise to the purest November sky their wonderful smooth or fluted domes – resents the avalanche disintegrating its former social coherence and funereal traditions. The invasion of foreigners has been brutal and incapable of assimilation: the unclear frontier between the living and the dead has to a large extent lost its seductive, exciting ambiguity.

Ever since my arrival in Cairo, after carefully taming the urban space, I have preferred to head to the southern macabre, the perimeter of which, approximately one kilometre long by a maximum two kilometres wide, extends, at the foot of the Citadel of Mehmet Ali and the look-out points of Al Muqattam, from the continuous hullabulloo of Bab al Qarafa to the quasi desert of the residential districts of Al Basatin (The Gardens). Described for centuries by foreign and indigenous writers, it was carefully drawn amongst others by Edward William Lane. Ibn Battuta stopped there and sketches a picture which, despite the passage of time, has not entirely lost its flavour: 'At Misr (Fosthath or old Cairo) one can see the cemetery of Al Qarafa, famous for its holiness (...) it belongs to the hill of Muqattam, which, according to divine promise, will be one of the gardens of Paradise. In Al Qarafa the inhabitants of Cairo erect beautiful chapels, surrounded by walls, that look like houses. They build residences close by and support readers who night and day melodiously recite the Koran. Some individuals construct *zawiyas* and *madrasas* next to the mausoleum. They spend Thursday night and Friday there with wives and children and walk in procession around the famous tombs. They also usually spend the night there from the 14th to the 15th of *chaaban*, whilst traders offer a wide range of repast'.

The City of the Dead has today a population of almost a million souls. They are born, grow, reproduce, multiply, age and die in the silent, condescending company of the deceased: it is a large minority, but a minority nevertheless who have taken refuge in the ancestral domain of death and developed, as I will have the opportunity to experience myself, a cultural and social life of their own, with its own norms, customs and rituals. I have not just seen burials in Al Khalifa: throughout an increasingly sweet, intoxicating sojourn, I attended weddings, parties, celebrations of circumcision and betrothal, family get-togethers, street football games. What began as an adventure and a challenge to myself, was gradually transformed into a haven, a yearning for possession: gradual appropriation of a space in which, thanks to the hospitality of the living and the immediacy of the dead, I finally felt tranquil and experienced a delicate merging of feelings of peacefulness, harmony and benevolence.

*   *   *

In modern Western society the thought of daily coexistence with death arouses a feeling of anguish and rejection. Our death rites are reduced to mere pretence: incapable of bridging the gap opened between the objective certainty of its mortality and the inner desire for some form of survival, our tormented consciousness cannot have recourse as in days of yore to the assimilating beliefs and ceremonies of backward communities.* Death is no longer accepted religiously or culturally as an integral part of our existence, it is a clandestine event behind the

---

* On the sociology of death in the West the reader can consult works by Jenkélevitch, Edgar Morin, Thomas, Bastide, Norman Brown, Ziegler, etc.

backs of the deceased and their social milieu. In metropolises like New York or Paris one can live for years without perceiving its troublesome intrusion. An efficient strategy of camouflage has whisked it out of sight, cleansed it from our language. Worse still; human beings have been deprived of their right to experience it as the natural outcome of a biological mutation. Stripped of its aura of dignity the corpse is set out like a dummy, an object of painful wrangling between family and rapacious funeral parlours. This illusory denial changes cemeteries into arenas of anxiety and terror, where the living penetrate furtively and run away at top speed: burials are a hollow social act, the momentary disturbing effect of which is diluted in inane bustle. A well-marked frontier separates necropolises from the rest of the urban space and transforms them into ghettoes or ghostly shrines. The price individuals pay for this shameful covering up of death is revealed in their inner vulnerability and ostrich-like attitude to the brutality of their condition: as in other terrains, the return of what has been cast out insidiously contaminates the substance of our lives.

To become acclimatised to a cemetery like Al Khalifa is to serve a healthy apprenticeship in the course of which the neophyte gradually sheds his worries and prejudices. Hardly glimpsed on my last visit to Cairo, it had symbolised in my eyes ever since the most distant boundary of unhappiness: the last most wretched suburb of a city whose monstrous growth condemned its children to disputing and snatching their territory from the deceased. After weeks of assiduous trawling, my impressions and ideas about it were modified. The City of the Dead is a colourful, fascinating urban agglomeration bursting with life, with districts which are ancient and modern, humble and aristocratic: the comfortable residences of the upper and middle classes run alongside enclaves and areas where poverty moves one to indignation. Traditionally inhabited by families settled next to their dead or by guardians of other people's mausolea, its population multiplied over the last decades with the arrivals of tens of thousands of Nubians forced to abandon their lands submerged by the Aswan dam and with a growing number of Cairenes fallen victim to the housing crisis and the unbearable promiscuity of the slum districts. As I soon saw, a great number of the settlers in Al Khalifa feel privileged and are proud to live there. In spite of the insufficient and haphazard urban infrastructure – the almost general absence of drainage, running water and, sometimes, electric light – they enjoy a space beyond the aspirations of millions of their co-citizens piled together in the housing blocks in the centre.

If, in contrast to Qait Bey, there has been only sporadic illegal occupation of pantheons, the laws of the property market impose their regulations in every sale, purchase or rental: speculation has sent sky-high the prices of the new mausolea built for the bourgeoisie become wealthy under Sadat. The concession of a lease or the safekeeping of a pantheon fetches very high sums, beyond the possibilities of most families. On one of my walks through Al Khalifa I came across the address of an estate agent, but my attempts at extracting a list of prices from him shattered against the wall of his stubborn suspicion: although I introduced myself as a Moroccan traveller in search of a home I was unsuccessful in sweeping aside his distrust of my hidden intentions. On the plots situated at the foot of Muqattam, it costs some 3000 pounds to excavate an underground tomb and the land is sold by the foot, as in housing developments in Giza and Masar al Guedid. However, a good number of the mausolea in Al Khalifa remain empty and can be examined at leisure through the bars of the outer gates.

The pantheons I just peered into and those I entered at the invitation of their residents represented a very varied range of styles and eras. Generally they comprise a stone-slab courtyard surrounded by rooms whose doors face onto a covered lobby or lead to an arcaded portico almost always decorated with verses or quotations from the Koran. Sometimes the tombs are raised to floor level and crowned with funeral memorial stones or stelas; others are hidden away in vaults whose architectural design, as I discovered later, corresponds to the one formed on the upper level by the home of the living; a narrow lobby at the foot of the stairs and two separate rooms for the corpses of both sexes. The patios are usually adorned with baskets of flowers and evergreen plants, and the walls display beautiful green tiles and Kufic inscriptions.

The wrought iron gates to other mausolea open onto gardens that have a wild abandoned look. The autumnal impression of decrepitude and negligence, the product of a perennial cycle of splendour and decline in bourgeois families, is intensified by those monuments erected to the eternal glory of their dead. The contrast between the original magnificence and the present state of ruin is a diaphanous illustration of this implacable process of degeneration which has always moved me as it has other writers. In one I glimpsed from the outside, someone had left a plate of seeds on top of a tomb – I am uncertain whether for its occupant or for all the wandering souls in the cemetery.

The precinct of inhabited pantheons makes up for the loss of this serenity through strange signs of life: clothes are hung out to dry across the arcades, gas stoves smoke, fowl peck and pets rest next to the tombs or cenotaphs. The majority of custodians or tenants that I met originated from Al Saaid, and stood out from their northern compatriots by virtue of their blackness and handsome features. Open and hospitable, the Nubians willingly invite strangers into their homes and offer them a glass of tea. Their progeny is usually numerous and their wives with faces uncovered hover discretely in the background during any visit. The men work as bricklayers or stone masons either building or repairing pantheons, but there are also many taxi-drivers, office-workers and clerks whose jobs oblige them to leave the maca- bre. Many youths are unemployed and live on the iron solidarity of the clan. Nevertheless, in these mixed areas of the cemetery, poverty never goes beyond the limits of what is tolerable.

The spectacle of twilight in Al Khalifa offers an impressive array of colourful, violent contrasts. Weak and bloodless, the sun appears to be bled white, behind the reddened silhouettes of minarets and mosque domes. The atmosphere is soaked in a strange luminosity. The terrestrial sphere repeats its round with a population that also rotates: the difference between living and dead, in parallel super-imposed layers in the mausolea, gradually fading into the shadows, is merely a question of time and degree.

*   *   *

The burial ceremonial in Al Khalifa has changed very little from the ones described by Lane.* The body of the deceased, carefully washed with soap and water, is wrapped in a *kefen* or green or white shroud before removal to its resting-place in an open coffin, usually covered over with a piece of linen. The eyes have been closed; ears and nostrils plugged with cotton wool; jaws tied with string to stop the mouth falling open on the journey; ankles strapped together; hands deco-rously laid on the chest. When the cortège leaves home and starts off, the faithful recite *azoras* from the Koran, relatives and friends run after the bier and take it in turns to carry it on their shoulders at a lively pace, as if in a relay race. This good deed or *hasana* is highly praisewor-thy, and everybody, including mere onlookers, reveals a desire to participate in order to enjoy the spiritual benefits. After the obligatory visit to one of the numerous mosques in Al Khalifa and the prayers of the Imam, the retinue walks or drives – depending on the distance to be covered and the social status of the deceased – to the mausoleum or tomb where he will be buried. The women walk behind and some-times burst out wailing and lamenting. Generally, upper-class burials

---

* E. V. Lucas, *Manners and Customs of the Modern Egyptians* (1863), East-West Publications, London 1978.

are silent and restrained. One of my occasional companions, to whom I commented this fact, just retorted ironically that the rich don't cry because they inherit money and property; the poor do because they are only left debts and expenses.

Thanks to my friend Ahmed, a master builder specialising in the construction of pantheons, I managed to examine the inside of one that had yet to enter service. A steep, narrow staircase, to be covered later with a stone slab, led to an underground granite sepulchre, oblong-shaped with a vaulted roof, comprising three rooms, a small lobby and two side-rooms, the entrance to which were adorned with Koranic verses and a simple indication as to the sex of their future occupants. On the outside, a similarly oblong-shaped cenotaph is usually set above the hypogea with the memorial stones or stelas decorated with lines from the Koran, stone turbans and the name and titles of the deceased. Ahmed explains to me that the corpses are deposited in the vault in the place corresponding to them, facing right towards the *qibla*. The funeral chambers must be spacious enough to allow the soul of the dead to be visited and examined by two angels named Naquir and Muncar. On the first night, the soul will experience the tension and anguish of their questioning, and this is consequently called *Lilat al Wahda* or Night of Solitude. Then, after the interrogation is complete, it will fly to the home of the just or the sinful to await the final judgment. According to other popular beliefs, the nomadic soul will wander throughout forty days, at the end of which mourning may be bid a definitive farewell on the occasion of the *Gumaa al Arbaain*.

On Fridays, the City of the Dead presents a striking spectacle of life and movement. A good number of Cairenes come to pray for their relatives and eat and rest in the pantheons. The sepulchres of those who have recently died are decorated with flowers or palm fronds. Some families set up a kind of canvas awning in the street, where the men receive condolences from their friends and drink a leisurely glass of tea. While the bourgeoisie, in shirt and tie or bejewelled, take refuge inside their mausolea, poor people usually spread themselves, their tablecloths and tea pots out by the side or on top of the tombs, welcoming inquisitive strangers and eager for distraction.

If the angels evoked by Ahmed only show themselves to the deceased, the goblins and demons that populate the cemetery do not always scorn the company of the living. One of my guides pointed out their wandering nocturnal presence in the area around Sayida Nafisa: they touched and even embraced the solitary walker, but vanished immediately God's name was invoked aloud. In the precinct of the pantheon looked after by his father, he added to convince me, one had taken up residence in the depths of a well. As I showed an interest in seeing the hiding place, he took me to see its keeper. Leaning on his crook, the old man hobbled up to the outer gate with a weighty bunch of keys. He was in his seventies and had an extraordinarily expressive face: his eyes shone astonishingly brightly and, after stunning the body of his interlocutor, seemed to disappear into infinity. Once informed of my whim – I confess that the idea of an exclusive interview with his demon was extremely attractive – he led me into a dirty poky corner, where a collection of objects was piled up; on the stone bench there was a circular hole covered over with a metal lid. He lifted it up and shouted down, the din echoed and resounded in the well for almost a minute. After making sure of the impact of this, he covered over the hole and, before taking me inside the mausoleum, locked the door to the cubby-hole inhabited by the *aafrit*. By night, he told me, he also closed the pantheon from the inside, to stop the demon from slipping through and disturbing his sleep. After a long struggle with his keys, the entrance was opened and we were in a kind of spacious, vaulted chapel in the centre of which was a large marble slab bare of decoration. The old man showed me the mess of blankets where he used to sleep, and invited me to share it with him if it appealed. I agreed and his face betrayed no sign of surprise.

Didn't my rest at his side perhaps satisfy the dark object of my desire? Was there any better cure or antidote against the anguish accumulated by the inevitable intrusions of Thanatos in my daily life? Did the fears that flourished insidiously under the wing of sleep – suffering, sickness, cancer, AIDS, old age – have a place within a mausoleum?

The motorways that gripped the City of the Dead were overflowing with cars, Cairo could be glimpsed in the distance with its lights and bustle, millions of people living the agony of their struggle to survive and I was enjoying, was able to enjoy with the old man a blissful, almost miraculous moment of peace. The journey on the dark night would become by his side more certain than the light of midday. Down secret steps, quite unintentionally, I had discovered once again in the macabre the mysterious fusion of St John of the Cross and Islam.

*   *   *

Obsidian approaches to the City of the Dead reserve for the besieger – even the Muslim besieger from elsewhere – infinite surprises. The profound internal coherence of the necropolis is revealed not suddenly but gradually, through successive perceptions and insights. Next to the areas of mausolea with patios and gardens are others where familiarity and immediacy with the deceased evoke even more powerfully the stubborn survival of millenary traditions. This promiscuous connivance is shot through with ancient customs of the Nile. The contiguity and unity of destiny between the dense collectivity of shadows and their ephemeral guests create bonds of complicity that are beneficial to both: the dead lose their profile of atavistic terror; the living are integrated into a world that will inexorably be theirs, but strengthened and soothed by such fruitful coexistence. Like other monotheistic religions, Islam has compromised with the pagan customs rooted in the peoples converted to its doctrine and has opted to assimilate them. The paintings and hieroglyphics on the hypogea of the Pharaohs reveal the daily life of the deceased with their relatives and servants. The expression on their faces is never sad: on the contrary, they appear radiant and calm.

Everything recalls the most pleasant aspects and scenes of life on earth: freed from his body, the deceased passes into his *ka*, that immaterial form or shadowy double that prolongs the human personality awaiting reincarnation. In its subterranean universe, the noctivagous soul enjoys not only food and drink but also the usual domestic comforts. The funereal inspiration of Al Khalifa has reflected from its beginning this ideal of bliss and harmony: the structure and conception of its hypogea is a palimpsest of the ancient beliefs of the Pharaohs. In upper Egypt and in rural areas, Nubians still place a symbolic offering of a loaf and a jug of water next to their tombs.

The sepulchres that jostle in the neighbourhood of the Al Qadriya district merge imperceptibly with wooden pavilions destined for family leisure and brick-built houses bristling with television aerials. The inhabitants of these mixed areas hang out their washing to dry between memorial stones and stelas, little children play at perching on top of them, hens peck around them, and the sight of a goat tied by a leg to the cenotaph of some *ulama* – whose *chahid* is crowned with an emblematic turban – does not shock too greatly. The sepulchres, like the houses, tend to be ochre in colour; but there are also plenty of lemon greens, and I have spotted some yellows, whites and oranges (only blue is rigorously excluded). Whoever zigzags among them hoping to lose himself discovers at every turn the remnants of previous visitations: rabbit hutches, pigeon lofts, flocks of sheep, a taxi waiting for its driver to have lunch, insolent Dodges and Volvos, a broken chassis. On the roof of a three-storey building, an extravagant advertisement for Canada Dry broadcasts the virtues of refreshment to a vast assembly of corpses. (Can the multinationals have decided to extend their range of influence into the afterlife?) The house-façades of those who have been on the pilgrimage to Mecca are brightly painted: naive drawings outline the boat or plane in which the owners travelled, the odd camel or palm tree, the black canopy hanging over the Muslim sanctuary of the Kaaba. At a bend in the street, fifty-odd people are celebrating with *yuyus* and applause the wedding of two children from the macabre: the bride is also sporting her Pronuptia model, and a taxi will not fail to take her and her husband for the compulsory photograph of the happy couple in front of the Hussein mosque. (I can already imagine the comic-sketch sweeper in his customary choreographic stance, energetically scattering the dust!)

The images of destitution in the poorest parts of the cemetery are quite similar to those I observed beyond its walls in the course of my stay in Cairo. The shops selling state-subsidised goods – oil, soap, beans, lentils, etc. – are under continuous siege from the mass of people who subsist thanks to official ration coupons. At the entrance to the mosque of Sayida Nafisa, the giving of alms to the needy by benefactors who sometimes come from smart residential areas in Mercedes provokes a riot: a flurry of women wrapped in black veils falls upon the driver encharged with distribution, they knock into each other; one of the women in mourning falls stunned to the ground in the midst of the uproar, but quickly picks herself up, like a footballer who realises that his pretence of injury has not drawn the referee's attention and that the game is going on without him. As a general rule, the inhabitants of Al Khalifa manage to endure their poverty with remarkable dignity: beggars are rare and the majority of families who invited me into their pantheon-houses reproachfully rejected my clumsy attempts to thank them for their welcoming glass of tea by leaving them a note. When I later got to know Ahmed and his family, the generosity with which he responded to my presents showed me the lengths to which the pride and nobility of a modest family of Nubians would go. My final evenings

with them touched me to the quick, bowled me over: all my precon-
ceptions about life in the cemetery were swept aside. If, as Jean Genet
wrote, '*la solitude des morts est notre gloire la plus certaine*', the solitude
the inhabitants of the macabre shared with them endowed my hosts
with supreme moral beauty: their love for their neighbour glowed
without expecting anything in return, as if awareness of the absolute
equality of men before death had abolished in its elementary
simplicity the loathsome barriers of power and money.

*   *   *

Will you ever return to Cairo?' I mutter on the flight back, after noting
that God the Father is enjoying a siesta with his cherubim on the
eiderdown of clouds. When, how, why?

To be present as the monster ever devours itself, as it implacably
gulps down its children? To spy on the final hecatomb, the violent
explosion of its entrails? To applaud the burning of the palaces of the
great? To be an impotent witness to the harsh survival of a people? To
sink into a Louis XXVI armchair and watch the latest television
creation?

At any rate, to keep my promise to Ahmed. To get a taxi on leaving
the airport and ask the driver to take me to Al Khalifa. A bedroom, a
patio, a garden: my familiar, hospitable pantheon in the City of the
Dead.

© Eberhard Hirsch, Círculo de lectores

About the Author

Juan Goytisolo is widely regarded as Spain's greatest living novelist and, simultaneously, her most trenchant critic. He has lived in voluntary exile since 1956.

Goytisolo was born in Barcelona in 1931. His father remained a supporter of Franco, despite the death of his wife in a Francoist air raid in 1938. Conflict with his father and the policies of the victorious Franco (whom he has described as his 'real, tyrannical father') furthered Goytisolo's radical tendencies and, after studying law at the universities of Barcelona and Madrid, he published his first novel in 1954. *Juegos de Manos* (The Young Assassins) received much acclaim, but Goytisolo rejected the censorious, oppressive climate of Francoist Spain and moved to Paris. There he worked for the publishing house Gallimard, bringing manuscripts to the company from Latin American authors such as Carlos Fuentes and Guillermo Cabrera Infante.

It was at Gallimard that Goytisolo met Monique Lange – the only person he says he has ever loved. Despite his growing awareness of his homosexuality, revealed to Lange in a letter of 1965, they continued living in Paris, married in 1978, and stayed together until her death in

1996. Goytisolo's sexual and artistic 'rebirth' is described in his autobiography, *Forbidden Territory* (1985) and *Realms of Strife* (1986).

Brought up in Catalonia and descended from Basque and Menorcan forbears, Goytisolo developed a literary Spanish to dynamite a language colonised by Fascism. His sympathy with minority peoples is evident throughout his work, and he has been declared an honorary Gypsy for his activities on behalf of that perpetually embattled race, while his support of the Cuban Revolution was tempered by disgust at Castro's persecution of African religions and homosexuals. Most apparent, especially in this collection, are his links with Islam, whose massive influence on medieval Spain and Spanish culture he constantly champions and celebrates.

Now over seventy, Goytisolo remains active as a novelist and a journalist, a political, cultural and sexual radical, a Socratic horsefly, continually out to sting the West for its complacency and narrowmindedness.

ELAND

61 Exmouth Market, London EC1R 4QL
Tel: 020 7833 0762   Fax: 020 7833 4434
Email: info@travelbooks.co.uk

Eland was started in 1982 to revive great travel books that had fallen
out of print. Although the list has diversified into biography and
fiction, it is united by a quest for the defining spirit of place. These
are books for travellers, readers who aspire to explore the world but
who are also content to travel in their mind. Eland books open out
our understanding of other cultures, interpret the unknown,
reveal different environments as well as celebrating the
humour and occasional horrors of travel.

All our books are printed on fine, pliable, cream-coloured paper.
Most are still gathered in sections by our printer and sewn as well
as glued, almost unheard of for a paperback book these days.
This gives larger margins in the gutter, as well as
making the books stronger.

We take immense trouble to select only the most readable books
and therefore many readers collect the entire series. If you
haven't liked an Eland title, please send it back to us saying
why you disliked it and we will refund the purchase price.

You will find a very brief description of all our books on the
following pages. Extracts from each and every one of them can be
read on our website, at www.travelbooks.co.uk. If you would
like a free copy of our detailed catalogue, please write
to us at the above address.

ELAND

'One of the best travel lists' WILLIAM DALRYMPLE

Memoirs of a Bengal Civilian
JOHN BEAMES
Sketches of nineteenth-century India painted with the richness of Dickens

A Visit to Don Otavio
SYBILLE BEDFORD
The hell of travel and the Eden of arrival in post-war Mexico

Journey into the Mind's Eye
LESLEY BLANCH
An obssessive love affair with Russia and one particular Russian

The Devil Drives
FAWN BRODIE
Biography of Sir Richard Burton, explorer, linguist and pornographer

Turkish Letters
OGIER DE BUSBEQ
Eyewitness history at its best – Istanbul during the reign of Suleyman the Magnificent

My Early Life
WINSTON CHURCHILL
From North-West Frontier to Boer War by the age of twenty-five

A Square of Sky
JANINA DAVID
A Jewish childhood in the Warsaw Ghetto and hiding from the Nazis

Chantemesle
ROBIN FEDDEN
A lyrical evocation of childhood in Normandy

Viva Mexico!
CHARLES FLANDREAU
A journey amongst the Mexican people

Travels with Myself and Another
MARTHA GELLHORN
Five journeys from hell by a great war correspondent

The Weather in Africa
MARTHA GELLHORN
Three novellas set among the white settlers of East Africa

Walled Gardens
ANNABEL GOFF
An Anglo-Irish childhood

Africa Dances
GEOFFREY GORER
The magic of indigenous culture and the banality of colonisation

Cinema Eden
JUAN GOYTISOLO
Essays from the Muslim Mediterranean

A State of Fear
ANDREW GRAHAM-YOOLL
A journalist witnesses Argentina's nightmare in the 1970s

Warriors
GERALD HANLEY
Life and death among the Somalis

Morocco That Was
WALTER HARRIS
All the cruelty, fascination and humour of a pre-modern kingdom

Far Away and Long Ago
W. H. HUDSON
A childhood in Argentina

Holding On
MERVYN JONES
One family and one street in London's East End: 1880–1960